WORKB

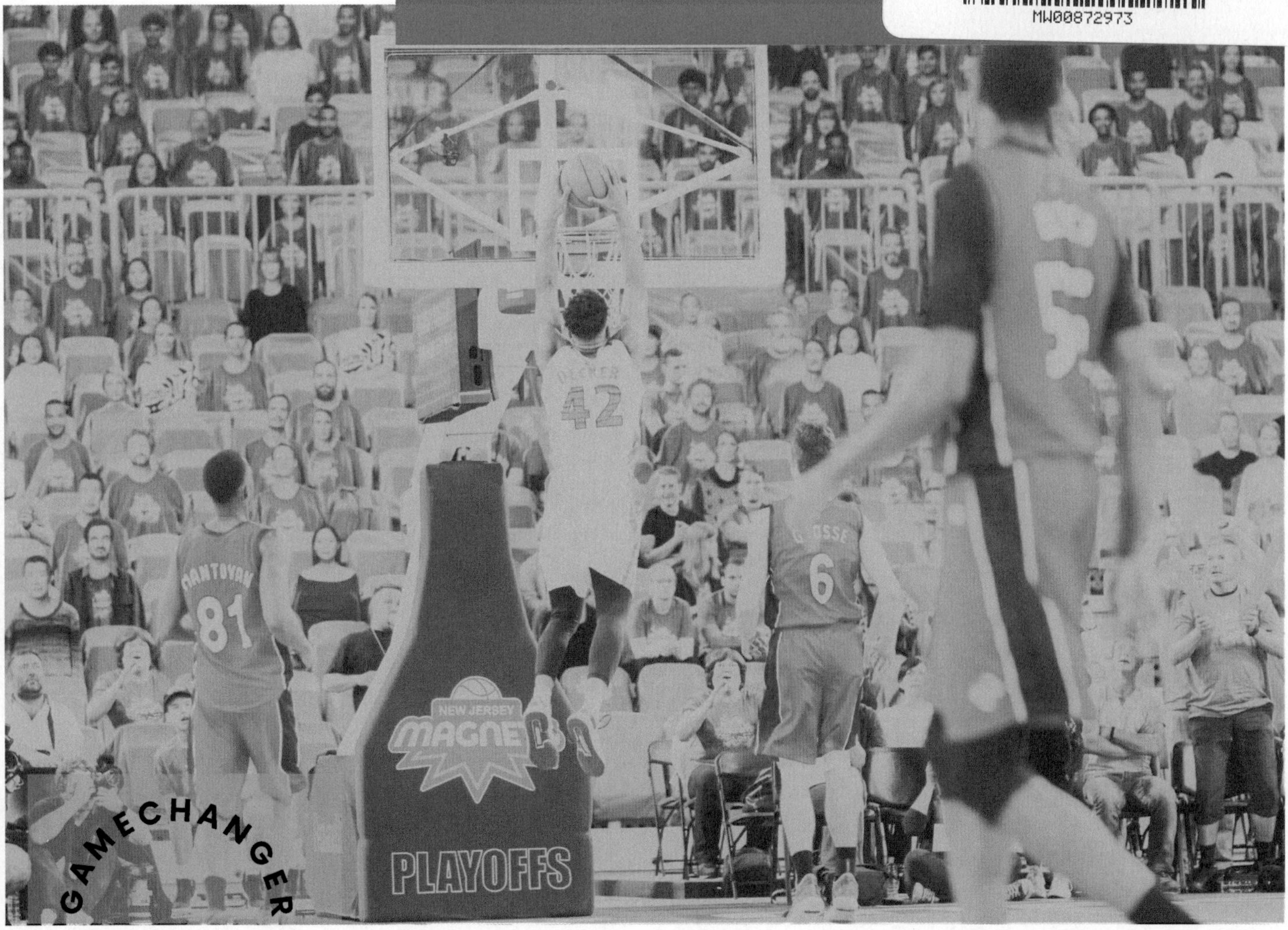

GAMECHANGER ATHLETES

GAMECHANGER ATHLETES MENTAL TRAINING WORKBOOK

APPLYING SPORT PSYCHOLOGY TOOLS & TECHNIQUES TO SUCCEED ON THE BASKETBALL COURT

DISCLAIMER

GameChanger Athletes Disclaimer

Contact Information

If you have any questions or requests regarding the use of this workbook or its content, please contact us at GameChanger Athletes.

contact@gamechangerathletes.org
www.gamechangerathletes.org

•

ABOUT GAMECHANGER ATHLETES

Our mission is to facilitate a holistic approach to developing athletes' character, mental well-being, and growth mindset. GCA is a nonprofit organization providing affordable services bringing equity and opportunity to all groups.

OUR APPROACH

Our approach applies scientifically supported methods and interventions from the field of sport and performance psychology to empower athletes in enhancing their mindset and mental performance. We provide athletes with a wide array of tools, resources, and exercises designed to cultivate essential skills. These skills include managing expectations, enhancing concentration, building confidence, effectively coping with mistakes, addressing perfectionism, managing social approval, developing pre-performance routines, handling pregame jitters, setting and achieving goals, overcoming the fear of failure, optimizing practice efficiency, recovering from injuries, fostering teamwork, and mastering emotional regulation, among other valuable techniques.

We trust that this workbook will empower you, offering valuable guidance and a range of tools to enhance your mindset and assist you in effectively navigating the challenges you face on your journey to training your mind and elevating your performance.

"When athletes of equal physical skills compete, the one with better mental skills WINS. "

TABLE OF CONTENTS

TABLE OF CONTENTS

CHAPTER 1

HOW TO MANAGE STRICT EXPECTATIONS

CHAPTER 1 OBJECTIVE

You'll learn how to uncover strict expectations that undermine your confidence and instead, focus on more manageable objectives.

WHAT YOU NEED TO KNOW

As you improve your game and have more success in basketball, expectations for your performance elevate. The problem is that high expectations can hurt your confidence when you fail to reach them. Playing with high expectations can lead to feeling more pressure to perform well.

> "Self-Confidence is how strongly you believe in your ability to execute your skill you train in practice every day."

For example, strict expectations such as, *"I must score 15 or more points in today's game"* or *"I shouldn't make any turnovers,"* cause you to judge how you are performing each play. You judge your game because you want to play up to a standard. Lastly, expectations can trigger frustration when you fail to achieve your high, strict expectations.

KEY POINT: Self-confidence and expectations are *different concepts and you don't want to mix these concepts.*

CHAPTER 1 – MANAGING EXPECTATIONS

Expectations are the absolute demands that you have about the quality of your performance or outcomes, such as, *"I SHOULD make 75% of my free throws."* These unwritten demands about how you *think you* **SHOULD** perform are often irrational. The problem is that super high expectations set up an unrealistic standard for your performance, which leads to judging your performance on every play during the game.

In contrast, self-confidence is how strongly you believe in your ability to execute your skills. When you have high confidence, you know you can perform and have no doubt about your ability to execute. With confidence, unlike expectations, you don't judge how you're doing when you perform.

> "I continually stress to my players that all I expect from them at practice and in the games is their maximum effort."
>
> — John Wooden

Types Of Expectations

You want to be aware of several types of expectations that might limit you, including:

1. Judgments about your statistics such as points per game, field goal percentage, free throw percent, etc.

2. Standards about the quality of your performance, such as how well or poorly you think you are performing or how it might look to others.

3. Demands about not making mistakes, such as turnovers, cheap fouls, forced shots, etc.

4. What you THINK others expect of you including teammates, coaches, parents, and fans.

Your first lesson is about managing harmful expectations or the "Formula for Success."

> **KEY POINT:** This formula is an important mental skill that you'll want to master first before moving on to other skills. When expectations are high, this can hold down confidence and lead you to feel frustration when you don't meet them.

YOUR MENTAL GAME FORMULA FOR SUCCESS

The formula helps you to flush out and discard expectations, so you can play freely with higher confidence. Instead of expectations, you want to perform with (1) high self-confidence and (2) focus on manageable process goals.

> "Focusing on small objectives, or process goals, during games helps you perform with a present, process focus."

Thus, focusing on small objectives (called process goals) during games helps you focus in the moment. Remember, you want to play each game without the pressure and judgments that come with strict expectations.

3 Steps in the Formula for Success

1. Uncover strict expectations (called "shoulds," "should nots," or musts) and commit to discarding your expectations.

2. Strive for high, stable confidence.

3. Focus on simple objectives that help you focus on the process.

What are Your Expectations?

Consider these questions to help you uncover expectations. Use the examples on the next page to help you answer these questions:

1. What expectations, such as, "I shouldn't get beat by the person I'm guarding." Do you place expectations on your performance?

2. What standards do you maintain about your performance, such as, "I **MUST** hit all my uncontested shots."

3. What do you demand of your game based on past experiences? For example, "We should beat this team, we always do" or, "I need to score 15 points because I did this against this opponent last time."

4. What standards have you set that cause you to feel upset or frustrated if you do not reach them such as zero turnovers, achieving a double-double, or holding the opponent you're guarding to single-digit points?

5. What names do you call yourself or adopt from others? Such as, "I'm a slow starter," or, "I'm a hot and cold shooter."

6. What past situations cause you to have generalizations about your current game? For instance, "I never perform well when this player guards me" or "I never shoot well in this gym."

7. What expectations do you think other people have for you, such as coaches, teammates, or parents? For instance, "*My coach expects me to be the leading scorer.*"

Here are a few examples of typical expectations for basketball players:

- I should score at least 15 points in the game.
- I should make defensive stops.
- I should make all of my free throws.
- I expect to make every uncontested shot.
- I should not make any mistakes.
- I should always make the right play.
- I shouldn't get scored on. I should not give up any turnovers.
- I can't give up any offensive rebounds.
- I have to get a certain number of rebounds or get a double every game.

You can use the examples listed in the table to help you complete Exercise 1.

Exercise 1: What Are Your Expectations?

In the table on the following page, you'll assess four areas of expectations you might have. Please place a check if you have the same expectations as the examples below. You may have expectations that aren't listed, write them in the "other expectations" box.

What are Your Expectations?

Example Expectations	✓
(1) Scoring, Outcomes, or Statistics: ▪ *"I should score 10 points or more per game."* ▪ *"I should shoot 50% or more from the field."* ▪ *"I should make all my open shots."* ▪ *"I should always score on a layup."*	
(2)The Qualify of My Performance: ▪ *"My performance should look and feel good."* ▪ *"I should always execute what my coach wants me to do."* ▪ *"I shouldn't miss any layups."* ▪ *"I shouldn't make any mistakes or very few."*	
(3)Mental Game: ▪ *"I should be focused all the time."* ▪ *"I should never get frustrated and be composed."* ▪ *"I should play with the same confidence I do in practice."*	
(4)What Others Expect of Me: ▪ *"My parents expect me to not make mistakes."* ▪ *"Coach expects me to be a leader and communicate with teammates."* ▪ *"My parents expect me to be a leading scorer on the team."* ▪ *"My teammates expect me to lead them or impact the game."* ▪ *"I should look like a star player for people in the stands."* ▪ *"Other people expect me to lead the team to victory."*	
Other Expectations:	

DISCARD EXPECTATIONS, FOCUS ON PROCESS GOALS

You want to stop striving to meet expectations, no matter if they are high or low. But how do you let go of expectations? (1) You stop judging your game. (2) You focus on small objectives in the moment-to-moment play, such as having good court awareness.

> "Stop focusing on striving for expectations, no matter if they're high or low ones."

Process goals help you:

1. Focus on executing a play, shot, pass, rebound, or steal.

2. Focus on the present moment, instead of thinking about future outcomes.

3. Focus on being decisive, confident, composed, and trusting your skills.

What are Effective Process Goals?

1. They are simple, usually NOT technical or related to technique during games.

2. They help you focus on executing your role successfully.

3. They help you focus on executing one play at a time, and not on the results.

4. They help you focus on what you want to do instead of avoiding failures or mistakes(i.e. "Don't make a turnover.").

In the Formula for Success, process goals help you focus on small objectives, such as seeing the court well. Process goals are not typical "goals" that you set for the season, but rather objectives to help you focus on the right performance cues. Performance cues are anything you need to think about or feel to help you execute a play.

EXAMPLE PROCESS GOALS

Following are a few examples of process goals to help you get started with thinking about process goals for your game.

First, what's your role on the team? And what are your objectives to help the team on offense and defense? Your objectives are specific to each task you execute. Please review the examples you can select from:

Offense:

- Focus on court awareness
- Know your plan with the ball
- Be decisive when shooting
- Keep feet moving on offense
- Get open for teammates
- Communicate with teammates
- Get feet set when setting screen
- Look for the open lanes

- Drive hard to the basket
- Setting picks for teammates
- End drives on balance

Defense:

- Focus on court awareness
- Focus on protecting my zone when on zone defense
- Be decisive on the steal attempt
- Anticipate the opponents' movement/play
- Keep feet moving on defense
- Focus on help defense
- Communicate with teammates
- Look for the steal or block opportunities
- Contest the shot decisively
- Hit the defender to box out for the rebound
- Stop the ball or defend the basket
- Focus on active feet
- Active eyes and head in your zone

Transition

- Hussle back on defense quickly
- Active eyes on sprint
- Get to my spot quickly
- Attack the basket quickly
- Communication with my teammates
- Look for the fast break on blocks, steals, shot attempts, and rebounds
- Get set up on offense quickly
- Attack before opponents can set up
- Be aware when we have a fast break

Shooting

- Get into space to receive the ball
- Call for the ball
- Be decisive with your shot
- Focus on the target
- Trust your shot technique

Rebounding:

- Box out your opponent
- Anticipate the shooter
- Be in the right position on court
- Time your jump with the rebound
- Chase the rebound
- Strong checkouts

Mental Process Goals:

- Keep my mind on the court only
- Be in the moment
- Trust my abilities/skills
- Let go of mistakes quickly
- Focus on tracking the movement of the ball
- Find tendencies of the other team
- Be aggressive on steals, blocks, or screens
- Be aware of game situations
- Play intuitively or athletically

Exercise 2: Focus on Process Goals, Not Expectations

Directions: Now it's your turn. Write examples of process goals—for each part of your game—that can help you focus on execution of one play at a time.

Think about what would help you perform better in your position if you focused more on a specific process goals or objectives. These might be the same objectives your coach wants you to think about.

> "Long term success is a direct
> result of what you achieve every day.
> Goals provide your daily routine."
>
> — Rick Pitino

What are Your Process Goals?

Process Goals by Task
Offense 1. 2. 3.
Defense 1. 2. 3.
Transition 1. 2. 3.
Mental Game 1. 2. 3.
Other 1. 2. 3.

SUMMARY

To perform with greater confidence and less pressure, you want to let go of meeting strict expectations. You do this by focusing on (1) high confidence and (2) small objectives or process goals. Identify and overcome your expectations and stop judging your performance, which will help you get into the flow of the game and feel more confident. This step alone will make a big difference in your mental game.

Keep in mind that you don't have to be perfect with "achieving" your process goals. And, you don't want your process goals to turn into expectations. They should help you think about executing one play at a time during the game. Note that your process goals may change each day depending on what you choose to focus on or want to improve in your game. The idea is that your game will improve by what you focus on, such as being more decisive on the ball.

Above all else, keep it simple. Set two process goals to focus on for offense and defense, such as good communication with teammates or having good footwork.

THIS WEEK'S ACTION PLANS

Please apply the mental strategies you learned this week to practice and games using the action plans below.

1. Awareness Exercise

Be aware of the expectations you have for your performance and the ones you feel from others before the next game. Make a note of your expectations and include them in your chapter answers for Exercise 1.

2. Practice Plan

Identify the most important process goals for your role on the team. Work on integrating one or two process goals or objectives into practices and scrimmages. Doing things like visualizing a play, being decisive, and trusting in your abilities during practice helps you focus on one play at a time instead of worrying about outcomes.

3. Game-Time Application

Prior to the game, set two process goals for both offense and defense. Make it a priority to focus on your process goals more so than thinking about meeting others' or your expectations for scores, results, or outcomes.

HABIT TRACKER

"Your habits will determine your future."

Instructions: List your top 5 process goals and check off or mark with an "X" each day you successfully complete the process goal in practice. At the end of the week or month, review your tracker. See which habits you consistently completed and where you might need to improve. Place your habit tracker in a location where you'll see it regularly, such as on your refrigerator, bathroom mirror, or locker-room. This visual reminder can help keep you accountable.

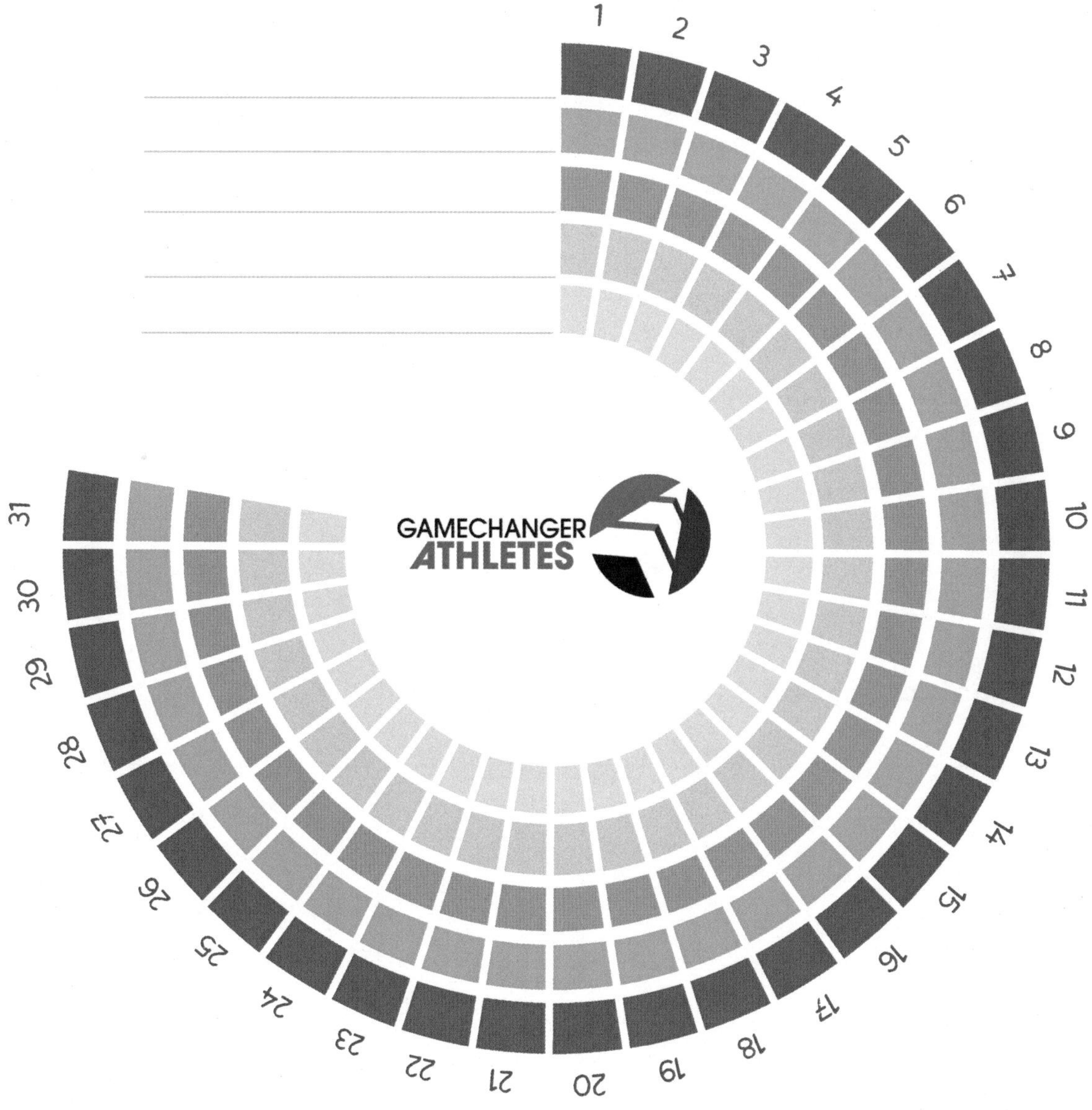

1 2 3 4 5 6 7 8 9 10 11 12 13 14 15 16 17 18 19 20 21 22 23 24 25 26 27 28 29 30 31

GAMECHANGER ATHLETES

POST-GAME ASSESSMENT FOR CHAPTER 1

After your next scrimmage or game, please answer a few questions about your mental game. It's best if you answer them on the same day as your scrimmage or game.

1. What are two things you did well today, in regard to your mental game and performance?

2. What are two things you would like to improve for the next game?

3. What expectations, if any, did you notice going into today's game?

4. What process goals did you focus on for today's game?

5. How well did you let go of your expectations and, instead, focus on your process goals?

6. What did you learn about replacing your expectations with process goals that will help youin the future?

MY NOTES

MY NOTES

MY NOTES

MY NOTES

CHAPTER 2

SHARPEN YOUR FOCUS

HOW TO FOCUS ON ONE POSSESSION AT A TIME

CHAPTER 2 OBJECTIVE

You'll learn how to focus on the process when playing, as well as learn how to refocus your mind when you're distracted.

WHAT YOU NEED TO KNOW

Good concentration means that you can focus in the moment and on the performance cues that help you perform. And if you're concentrating well, you can overcome distractions by getting your mind back into the game quickly.

"If you're concentrating well,
you can overcome distractions quickly."

Focusing on the process means:

1. Thinking only about the present moment (here and now), not the last possession or thinking ahead.
2. Thinking about "one play, point, or possession at a time."
3. Focusing only on executing your role, not thinking ahead about the outcome or your statistics for the game.

To get into the flow of the game, you have to be able to react to what's happening in the moment. If you dwell on making a turnover, you have a split focus between the past and the current play. And thinking about future outcomes, such as *"I hope coach will be happy with my game today"* or *"I need to score 10 points today,"* takes your focus away from the process during a game.

FOUR STEPS FOR FOCUSING ON THE PROCESS

Here are the steps to help you focus in the moment or have a process focus:

1. Know the performance cues for your position on the team (You may have already done a lot of this with process goals in chapter 1).

2. Uncover your most common distractions that hurt concentration. Be aware when you are distracted or thinking ahead.

3. Immerse your mind into your performance cues one possession at a time. You can use your process goals to help you focus on executing one play at a time (Plan A for Focusing).

4. Use the 3 R's to help you refocus (Plan B for Focusing) to help you get back to the present moment.

PERFORMANCE CUES AND CONCENTRATION

Performance cues are thoughts, images, or feelings that help you plan and execute a play, such as court awareness (knowing where everyone is on court). Step One asks you to know the performance cues for your position. For example, if you're a center forward, you think about your position on the court, stay under the basket, grab rebounds, score points from the paint, and block out opponents for rebounds, and create lanes for teammates' drives.

Next, you want to notice when you get distracted or think about non-relevant stuff. For example, it hard to think about your job if you're thinking about who's in the stands. Thinking about the stands takes your mind away from focusing 100% on the court. Dealing with distractions, such as taunting or crowd noise, is part of being an athlete. You just don't want distractions to lead to mental mistakes.

What performance cues help you execute your position well when on offense and defense?

> "Just think about the basketball game.
> If you start to think about who is going to win the championship, you've lost your focus."
>
> — Michael Jordan

Performance cues overlap with process goals, but can be more detailed. Below are a few examples for different parts of your game.

Example Performance Cues

Offense Cues

- Focus on court awareness or seeing the court well
- Focus on spacing or position on court
- Know the set play or type of offense running
- Be decisive when shooting
- Keep mind on the court when playing
- Get open for teammates
- Communicate with teammates
- Set screen early with correct position

- Look for the open lanes
- Drive hard to the basket

Defense Cues:

- Focus on court awareness
- Be aggressive during half-court presses
- Focus on protecting your zone on when playing a zone D
- Understand your assignment
- Be decisive on the steal attempt
- Anticipate the opponents' movement/play
- Keep feet moving on defense
- Backup or support teammates
- Communicate with teammates
- Look for the steal or block opportunities
- Contest the shot decisively
- Block out person you are guarding and box out for the rebound

Transition Cues

- Hustle back on defense quickly
- Know my spot or route
- Anticipate the outlet pass

- Communicate with my teammates
- Look for the fast break on blocks, steals, and rebounds
- Attack before opponents can set up
- Get set up on offense quickly
- Be aware when team has a fast break opportunity

Shooting Cues

- Be aware of positioning
- Cut to get open for the shot
- Call for the ball
- Receive the ball into your hands
- Be decisive when you have the opening
- See the target (rim)
- Square up; Elevate for the shot
- Trust your shot (react to the target)

Passing

- Be aware of teammates
- Look for space; Create a lane for the pass
- Decide on the type of pass (bounce, chest, overhead)
- See the pass in your mind

- Focus on teammate
- Move towards receiver
- React and trust

STEP 1: DEFINE YOUR PERFORMANCE CUES

Your position and role on the team will dictate performance cues. For example, if you play point guard, your role is to coordinate the team, run the play call, communicate with teammates, and handle the ball.

Performance cues are what you focus on to execute your role on the team and your skills.

KEY POINT: Keep in mind that what you focus on during games will differ from the performance cues during practice because in practice you're trying to learn and improve skills. In games, you're relying on what you have already learned from practice and playing intuitively.

EXERCISE 1: WHAT ARE PERFORMANCE CUES?

In the table below, list the performance cues for your role on offense, defense, transition, and shooting. Think about what your coach wants you to focus on — without being technical. This exercise is similar to defining your process goals or objectives you completed in chapter 1.

Table on the next page...

What are Your Performance Cues?

Sports Tasks	Performance Cues for Each Task
Task 1 (Offense)	1. 2. 3. 4.
Task 2 (Defense)	1. 2. 3. 4.
Task 3 (Transition)	1. 2. 3. 4.
Task 4 (Shooting)	1. 2. 3. 4.

STEP 2: YOUR COMMON DISTRACTIONS

What are your common distractions during games or practice? You can think of distractions in two ways... Distractions can start internally or externally. Internal distractions come from your own thinking, such as, *"I hope coach doesn't pull me if I keep missing."* External distractions start from the environment or other people. Below are some examples of common distractions or task-irrelevant cues.

Internal and External Distractions

Internal Distractions	External Distractions
▪ Thinking you need to win	▪ Hearing your coaches yell
▪ Worrying about disappointing others	▪ Seeing your friends at the game
▪ Thinking about who's watching you perform	▪ Hearing parents yell in the stands
▪ Over-analyzing your technique or form	▪ Teammates yelling after a mistake
▪ Wondering what to do after the game	▪ The other team trash-talking
▪ Thinking about the last play or game	▪ Temperature of the gym
▪ Thinking about the next half of the game	▪ Poor court conditions
▪ Imagining a poor outcome (Don't miss...)	▪ Bad calls by the referee
▪ Dwelling on a past mistake	▪ Lack of grip or air in the balls
▪ Thinking about what to do after game	▪ An opponent that cheats

EXERCISE 2: WHAT DISTRACTS YOU?

What are your common distractions, such as thinking about your stats? You can pick ones from the table above or think about other ones that may affect your focus on the court.

> "Sometimes in the past when I played something might make me lose focus, or I would go home after a game where I thought I could have played better and I would let it hang over my head for a long time when it shouldn't."
>
> — Lebron James

Table on the next page...

What are Your Distractions?

Type of Distraction	Your Distraction
External Distractions (Ex: fans, teammates, parents in stands):	1. 2. 3.
Past Distractions (Ex: mistakes, poor play, thinking about last point):	1. 2. 3.
Future Distractions (Ex: game stats, outcomes, what you are doing after competition):	1. 2. 3
Random Distractions (Ex: what you had for lunch, relationships, school work):	1. 2. 3.

STEP 3: FOCUS ON EXECUTION ONLY

When you are focusing well, you're into the flow of the game. This means you are only thinking about your performance cues when playing. Using process goals (see chapter 1) helps you with this task because performance cues are often one and the same. However, process goals are typically the cues you select to focus on during the game, such as being decisive when shooting. Whereas, performance cues are the entire universe of what's important including position on the court, teammates, the play, what defense your opponents are running and so forth, for example.

You can start by thinking about the objectives that will help you perform your position. Also, you want to simplify your thinking to get into the zone and thus play intuitively.

KEY POINT: Remember, what you focus on, you improve. If you want to be more decisive when shooting, focus on doing this in games. Make it a small goal or objective in the game.

"What you focus on, you improve."

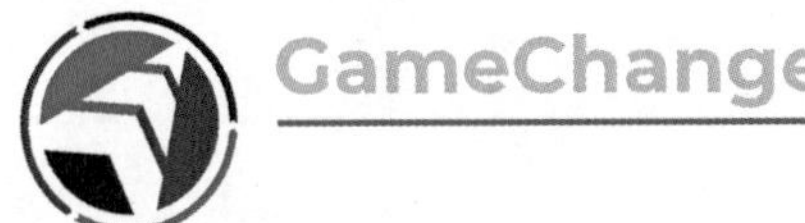

STEP 4: USE THE THREE R'S TO REFOCUS

The Three R's for refocusing helps you shift your focus as quickly as possible after a distraction. Plan B is to refocus quickly when distracted. This is Plan B because it's intended to be a backup to Plan A. The sooner you can refocus after your mind wanders, the better your concentration.

The Three R's for Refocusing include:

1. **Recognize** — Notice when you are distracted or not focused in the moment.
2. **Regroup** — Interrupt your thought process so you can start refocusing.
3. **Refocus** — Change your focus to performance cues in the moment.

KEY POINT: Ask yourself: "What should I focus on right now to execute this play, run, shot, or defense?" Your answer identifies what's important to think about.

EXERCISE 3: PRACTICE USING THE THREE R'S

Directions: *In the table below, using your common distractions you defined earlier, write a regroup and refocus statement for each.*

Regroup & Refocus Statements

Distraction	Regroup	Refocus
I'm thinking about the last mistake I made.	Stop! That's over. Thats' not important.	W.I.N (What's Important Now) Focus on the next play **ONLY**!
1.		
2.		
3.		
4.		

REFOCUS QUICKLY

During play, you must refocus quickly because of the pace of play. Refocusing should only take one to two seconds to complete. Think of this as shifting your focus back to the current play. In this case, you use a quick three-R's approach.

You'll want to "practice" your refocusing skills often. You can do this in your training, practice, or in your life as well. Practice refocusing during practice when you become distracted by mistakes, your coach yelling, or your teammates talking.

Other Strategies to Improve Concentration

1. **Become the warrior athlete** - Enter the role of a focused athlete. Leave your worries or distractions from your life at home or "park" them in the parking lot. Commit to focusing on the game for the next two hours or length of the game starting with your warm up. Write down anything that is on your mind and commit to parking it. You can come back to it after the game.

2. **Have a positive intention** or focus on what to do instead of what you want to avoid doing (e.g., thinking about making a shot instead of don't miss). Move from avoidance thinking to success thinking.

3. **Remind yourself that focusing on the process** brings about desired outcomes! Focus on one possession or basket at a time, not the score, statistics, or outcomes.

4. **Center yourself with a breath-grounding technique**. Direct your attention to your breath. Take 3 deep, deliberate breaths. Try inhaling for 2-4 seconds and exhaling for 4-6 seconds. Find your ideal rhythm, ensuring your exhale matches or exceeds your inhale. This technique brings oxygen to your brain and bloodstream. Aiding you in disengaging from distracting thoughts, increasing focus & decreasing stress.

REFOCUS QUICKLY

Other Strategies to Improve Concentration

5. **Create a focus list- controllables list**. As you prepare for your game (ideally, 2 hours before, the night before, or during the week leading up to it), grab a pen and paper. Here's a powerful exercise to help you streamline your focus:

- Write down everything you're worried about, big or small, regarding the game.
- Now, go through your list and **cross out** anything you cannot control. These might include court conditions, officiating decisions, others' opinions, or how your teammates will perform, how many shots you will make, etc.)
- What you have left are the elements within your control. Concentrate your attention on these remaining factors. These are the areas where you can make a real difference.

6. **Find a focal point:** Focus your vision on a specific spot (the smaller and more specific the better). For example, a crack in the wall, a spot on the backboard, the dot on the free-throw line, or youetc. And let this be an anchor or the place you look at to regain focus when you are distracted or faltering. Prior to competition establish your focal point and and cue words to recite when you look at the focal point. For example, stay aggressive lock in, you got this, etc.

CONCENTRATION GRID EXERCISE

The Concentration Grid exercise serves as a crucial tool to boost your present-moment focus and increase awareness of distractions. The grids are a series of scrambled numbers from 00-99 (some are 1-100) on a page. The goal is to cross off consecutive numbers in numerical order from 00 -99. Initially, this exercise can be a tad frustrating, but patience is key to improvement.

Start by recording the time it takes to complete the grid – this serves as your baseline. Challenge yourself to reduce your completion time each chapter.
We recommend integrating this exercise into your routine, ideally 4-5 days a week. It's versatile; you can practice at home, before training, or during free moments.

Begin in a quiet setting to familiarize yourself with the process and to monitor your focus on the present. Once you master the grid within 5 minutes or less in a quiet environment, level up. Add music, introduce distracting sounds, or complete the task in front of the TV to simulate game-like interruptions. You can find additional concentration grids online at www.concentrationgrids.com/grids

Benefits of the concentration grid:

- Increase your ability to maintain focus through distractions.
- Improve the duration of your focus concentration and attention spans.
- Develop a "mental monitor" that helps you recognize when you lose focus or distraction triggers.
- Build your capacity for self-regulation - the ability to stay calm and focused under stressful, pressure situations. And help you detect when you're pushing too hard and need to pause, take a breath, and regain optimal focus.

Concentration Grid Exercise on *page 20-24*.

Reminder: Maintaining a record of your completion times is essential for gauging progress. Utilize the Concentration Grid Time Journal provided on ***page 25*** to effectively track your improvements.

SUMMARY

Every athlete has learned to concentrate in sports, but distractions are inevitable in basketball. Your goal is to keep your mind on the court, one play at a time. This means staying in the moment and refocusing quickly when distracted. You'll also want to note your own common distractions, so you can refocus quickly.

"*Refocus*" is your buzzword for today's lesson. When concentrating well, you don't pay attention to distractions because you're only thinking about your performance cues. However, at times you will lose focus and must refocus quickly on the fly. Don't allow distractions to run wild in your mind and lead to making mistakes.

THIS WEEK'S ACTION PLANS

Please apply the mental strategies you learned this week to practice and games using the action plans below.

1. Awareness Exercise

Keep a journal of you common distractions (internal and external) during practice and competition. Notice any patterns when distracted, such as if you tend to think about outcomes more than dwell on past mistakes.

2. Practice Plan

Using your common distractions, make a refocus statement (using the Three R's) for each distraction. Memorize each refocus statement at home and practice rehearsing them. You can use mental rehearsal to imagine yourself in a game or practice refocusing when distracted.

3. Game-Time Application

Focus only on your performance cues for offense and defense. Remind yourself to focus on one possession at a time. If you become distracted, use your Three R's. Be ready to refocus as you will get distracted at times. As a matter of fact, refocusing quickly can be a process goal for the game.

POST-GAME ASSESSMENT FOR CHAPTER 2

After your next scrimmage or game, please answer a few questions about your mental game. It's best if you answer them on the same day as your scrimmage or game.

1. What are two things you did well today with your mental game and performance?

2. What are two things you would like to improve for the next game?

3. How successful were you in focusing in the moment and not thinking too far ahead or about a past play?

4. At what times did you become distracted during the game? What were the triggers for your distractions?

5. Were you successful using the Three R's when you were distracted?

6. How well did you focus on your process goals today to help you stay in the present?

7. What did you learn about the mental skill of focus that you can apply to future games?

CONCENTRATION GRID

The point of power is always in the present moment. - Louise Hay

Instructions: In this exercise, your goal is to consecutively mark off numbers in numerical order, either from 00 to 99 or in reverse from 99 to 00. It's crucial to emphasize that skipping numbers is not allowed. And, remember to keep track of your time as you complete the exercise.

24	39	45	36	66	3	49	76	61	78
60	5	57	31	95	85	21	68	52	7
12	22	23	25	44	87	29	77	67	35
96	55	82	100	58	14	80	9	10	53
71	81	4	69	40	19	99	92	20	13
84	50	2	42	62	73	64	34	27	8
28	17	46	93	65	37	33	98	26	94
1	70	43	16	32	30	59	86	97	56
88	72	79	90	91	47	75	74	63	48
11	51	6	83	89	41	54	38	18	15

CONCENTRATION GRID

The point of power is always in the present moment. - Louise Hay

Instructions: In this exercise, your goal is to consecutively mark off numbers in numerical order, either from 00 to 99 or in reverse from 99 to 00. It's crucial to emphasize that skipping numbers is not allowed. And, remember to keep track of your time as you complete the exercise.

79	54	84	39	45	70	82	89	63	91
98	71	78	50	35	43	19	12	90	36
44	59	67	40	20	69	94	22	14	93
86	10	32	95	97	2	87	66	48	51
52	55	57	58	42	41	33	11	85	1
73	60	17	26	34	68	5	80	9	99
38	13	7	47	96	92	75	28	6	23
4	24	21	100	64	74	53	72	25	65
31	88	29	83	27	77	61	15	56	76
49	3	8	81	46	16	18	37	30	62

CONCENTRATION GRID

The point of power is always in the present moment. - Louise Hay

Instructions: In this exercise, your goal is to consecutively mark off numbers in numerical order, either from 00 to 99 or in reverse from 99 to 00. It's crucial to emphasize that skipping numbers is not allowed. And, remember to keep track of your time as you complete the exercise.

64	42	21	62	24	90	56	14	81	19
48	88	43	76	46	78	1	63	58	60
85	11	79	50	34	71	28	80	94	99
86	47	12	27	83	8	37	33	10	41
39	95	65	75	89	55	45	70	100	13
91	25	59	66	57	6	74	53	87	61
38	68	35	97	17	52	73	54	30	51
32	31	9	3	7	96	22	4	93	82
36	26	2	23	16	77	67	98	92	49
84	29	40	20	69	72	15	5	44	18

CONCENTRATION GRID

The point of power is always in the present moment. - Louise Hay

Instructions: In this exercise, your goal is to consecutively mark off numbers in numerical order, either from 00 to 99 or in reverse from 99 to 00. It's crucial to emphasize that skipping numbers is not allowed. And, remember to keep track of your time as you complete the exercise.

66	36	33	82	80	35	61	34	62	41
95	37	5	51	45	71	91	52	9	44
28	38	19	20	29	63	92	24	46	8
48	1	18	74	40	16	25	43	67	94
42	55	13	59	90	56	84	87	4	76
81	70	3	83	96	53	73	12	65	85
39	31	100	58	30	72	75	54	21	68
98	14	97	27	10	78	17	47	15	6
93	50	99	89	26	7	86	77	79	2
49	32	11	64	22	60	57	88	23	69

CONCENTRATION GRID

The point of power is always in the present moment. - Louise Hay

Instructions: In this exercise, your goal is to consecutively mark off numbers in numerical order, either from 00 to 99 or in reverse from 99 to 00. It's crucial to emphasize that skipping numbers is not allowed. And, remember to keep track of your time as you complete the exercise.

44	22	14	72	94	52	34	89	49	7
95	16	2	78	86	70	87	79	18	46
80	25	58	13	92	5	10	32	12	50
91	65	84	45	9	40	100	77	85	26
1	37	96	20	64	53	62	51	29	8
57	54	4	98	63	6	97	17	83	3
21	28	33	36	99	61	90	15	48	75
31	81	73	67	66	35	71	30	74	39
82	43	19	41	24	88	93	11	76	60
27	42	56	55	68	47	38	69	23	59

Concentration Grid Time Journal		
Date	**Completion time**	**Notes:** List distractions you observed, how you responded when frustrated, & best practices that helped you refocus or maintain focus.

MY NOTES

MY NOTES

MY NOTES

MY NOTES

CHAPTER 3

BUILD SELF-CONFIDENCE

HOW TO HAVE PROACTIVE CONFIDENCE

CHAPTER 3 OBJECTIVE

To learn how to have "proactive confidence" prior to every game or scrimmage. And to develop stable confidence during play.

WHAT YOU NEED TO KNOW

Self-confidence is the belief in your ability to execute basketball skills. Confidence gives you the mental edge to perform consistently at your best. High confidence also helps you brush off mistakes easily, perform with less fear, and stay calm and composed more easily.

When playing with high confidence, you take more risks and play aggressively instead of tentatively. Finally, confidence helps you trust in the skills that you practice every day.

> "Confidence help you trust in the skills that you practice every day."

Confidence in basketball comes from many months and years of practicing and playing in games. You get confidence from the sum of past success, practice, agility training, conditioning, performing well under pressure, and mental toughness. Knowing you have the physical skills and talent to perform well helps you feel confident.

KEY POINT: Proactive confidence is learning how to bring a high level of confidence to the start of each game. Reactive confidence is waiting until your performance shines before you can feel confident.

You'll improve confidence by focusing on these two areas:

1. Learn how to be proactive with confidence instead of reactive.

2. Understand and overcome the top confidence killers (see woorkbook 3B).

SOURCES OF CONFIDENCE

You gain confidence in many ways (see the table below on sources of confidence). Use this table to help you complete Exercise 1.

EXERCISE 1: WHAT ARE YOUR SOURCES OF CONFIDENCE?

What things help you feel confident in basketball? In the table below, place a check next to your top 10 sources of confidence. Please add other sources that are not listed in the table below.

Table on the next page...

Top 10 Sources of Confidence

Sources of Confidence	✓	Sources of Confidence	✓
Past success in basketball or sports		Pregame mental preparation	
Consistent practice and drills		Studying the opponents	
How well you perform in games		Mental game coaching	
Positive comments from others		Performing well under pressure	
Supportive people in your life		Positive rapport with teammates	
Additional training outside of practice		Proper nutrition & hydration	
Quality coaching		Fitness level or conditioning	
Belief in your physical talent		Supportive parents or friends	
Good technique or form		Pregame mental rehearsal	
High basketball IQ		How good the opposing team is	
Having an effective warm-up routine		Comfortable with court	
Other Sources:			

EXERCISE 2: AREAS OF CONFIDENCE YOU CAN CONTROL

What sources of confidence can you directly control from the areas you selected in Exercise 1 above? For example, practice, belief in your skills, and fitness are all under your control.

Conversely, what others say, the opponents, referees, and playing at home or away is not under your control.

Your goal is to focus on the sources of confidence that you can control. Using the sources of confidence that you listed from the preceding table, which sources of confidence are directly in your control? List them here.

Sources of Confidence Under My Control

1. ______________________________

2. ______________________________

3. ______________________________

4. ______________________________

5. ______________________________

You, not other people, are responsible for feeling confident—that's why it's called SELF-confidence. Self-confidence comes from the belief in your skills to play the game, not from what others say about your game. For example, teammates, the court conditions, opponents, or referees should not influence your confidence. If so, influences outside of your direct control affect how confident you feel during play.

PROACTIVE AND STABLE CONFIDENCE

You want to think about these two areas to improve self-confidence:

1. Proactive confidence is your ability to fuel your confidence prior to competition. Take responsibility for feeling confident before you play or perform.

2. Stable confidence is keeping your confidence at the same level during game. With stable confidence, you don't let bad breaks, calls, or mistakes hurt confidence.

Stable confidence is based on weeks, month, and years of practice, learning, and competing in basketball--and other sports you might have played. How many years have you been playing basketball? That's how long you've been working on your confidence.

> "Confidence is a tangible thing; it comes from practice and repetition. You have to put in the work in order to build that confidence. When others see you have that confidence, they will gravitate around you and have confidence in you. But it starts with you."
>
> — Kobe Bryant

EXERCISE 3: YOUR CONFIDENCE RÉSUMÉ

Proactive confidence is fueling your confidence prior to the game. One way to do this is to write a confidence résumé, which includes your past successes or accomplishments, past experiences, strengths of your game, and anything else that helps you feel confident.

Use the questions below to help you get started and write your confidence résumé below:

1. What are your talents, abilities, or strengths as a basketball player?

2. What do others think you're good at (e.g., your technique, your commitment, determination, ability to overcome adversity, etc.)?

3. What have you accomplished in basketball that you are proud of (e.g. state championship, awards, great performances in games, etc.)?

4. How would you describe your game to others if you took the most positive stance possible?

5. What can you say about how your practice that gives you confidence?

6. What can you say about your commitment or work ethic in sports?

7. What can you say about the coaching you receive that helps you feel confident?

8. What can you say about your mental game that gives you confidence in your ability?

9. What can you say about training routines that you use outside of regular practice that gives you confidence?

MY CONFIDENCE RÉSUMÉ

In the space provided below, write your confidence résumé for each area that applies.

Physical Abilities or Talents (speed, strength, hand-eye, etc.):

1. ______________________________
2. ______________________________
3. ______________________________
4. ______________________________
5. ______________________________

Strengths Stated by Others (coaches, parents, other players)?

1. ______________________________
2. ______________________________
3. ______________________________
4. ______________________________
5. ______________________________

Past Accomplishments (awards, improvement, part of championship teams, etc.):

1. ______________________________
2. ______________________________
3. ______________________________
4. ______________________________
5. ______________________________

Describe Your Game in The Most Positive Way:

1. ______________________________
2. ______________________________
3. ______________________________
4. ______________________________
5. ______________________________

Practice, Training, Coaching, or Additional Training:

1. ____________________
2. ____________________
3. ____________________
4. ____________________
5. ____________________

Your Mental Game Strengths:

1. ____________________
2. ____________________
3. ____________________
4. ____________________
5. ____________________

Diet, Fitness, or Nutrition:

1. ____________________
2. ____________________
3. ____________________
4. ____________________
5. ____________________

Task-Specific Area (i.e., shooting, rebounding, running plays, etc.):

1. ____________________
2. ____________________
3. ____________________
4. ____________________
5. ____________________

What to do with your confidence resume? You'll want to memorize and review your confidence résumé prior to games to remind yourself why you deserve to feel confident. Print it out and put it in your bag or send it to your phone and save it for review. Keep your confidence résumé up to date and add to it by asking others to help you.

KEY POINT: Real confidence comes from the inner belief in your skills, not what others say or do. Confidence must start on the inside based on years of practice and play.

PROACTIVE, CONFIDENT SELF-TALK

Most ball players have an internal voice called "self-talk." Your self-talk can help you feel confident, "I enjoy the challenge of a close game," or hurt confidence, "We can't win a close game in the last two minutes."

Using proactive, positive self-talk before a game can help you fuel your confidence level.

EXERCISE 4: COMPARE YOUR SELF-TALK

Please compare your self-talk when you perform well versus poorly. What's the difference in your self-talk? In the tables on the next page, place a checkmark next to the statements that match your self-talk. Use "other" in the space provided for additional self-talk.

> "Confidence is everything in this game, if you don't think you can, you won't!"
>
> —Jerry West

Table on the next page...

Your Negative Self-Talk

Negative Self-Talk	✓
1. *"Wow, I stink today! What is wrong with me?"*	
2. *"Here I go again, missing shots early. My game is off today."*	
3. *"I am a horrible athlete, I should give up and walk away from the game."*	
4. *"I'm never going to be a starter, I just need to quit now."*	
5. *"I should find another sport after my performance today."*	
6. *"I'm going to get benched if I turn the ball over again."*	
7. *"How can I miss that easy shot? That's awful!"*	
8. *"My defense is horrible, I can't cover anyone."*	
Other:	

Your Self-Talk When Playing Well	✓
1. *"I am a great ball player and have all the skills."*	
2. *"I feel like I am well prepared. I've put in the work."*	
3. *"I can take on anyone one-on-one."*	
4. *"I am fast, strong and confident in my skills."*	
5. *"I can do this! I've proved it to myself. I deserve to play well."*	
6. *"I am focused and in control."*	
7. *"My shot it on, I can't miss today!"*	
Other:	

EXERCISE 5: SELF-TALK TO BOOST CONFIDENCE

You can use proactive self-talk to feel more confident. Pick one part of your game, such as passing, shooting, or man-to-man defense. First, what do you think when playing well? For example, you might think, "If I see a lane, I am going to attack the basket," or if have an open shot, you might say, "I can hit this shot, trust my shot."

List five self-talk statements you can use to help you take control of your confidence.

HINT: Think about what you say to yourself when you feel superior confidence. For example, "I'm going to nail this three-point shot." Keep your statements short.

Write Your Confident Self-Talk Here

1. ____________________

2. ____________________

3. ____________________

4. ____________________

5. ____________________

You can use self-talk during your pregame warm-up or during plays. You should memorize and rehearse these statements before your next game.

REHEARSE YOUR PERFORMANCE

You can also be proactive with confidence by using pregame mental rehearsal or visualization. This is a very natural skill for many athletes. Think about it as imagining yourself playing great ball.

> "Be aware of when you're 'mind reading' into what others MIGHT think about your game"

Do you imagine or daydream about performing well and making plays with confidence prior to the game? What can you rehearse in your mind before a game? You can rehearse:

1. Making plays in your role or position on the team.

2. Specific skills you want to execute with such as shooting or defending.

3. A mental "highlight reel" of your best plays from past games.

4. Playing with a strong mental game, such as being aggressive and decisive.

5. Coping with adversity, such as taunting, bad calls from referees, or mistakes.

When should you rehearse your performance? The best time is pregame: in the locker room or on the court during your warm-up. I suggest you use a first-person perspective and experience yourself as if you are on the court playing the game from your own eyes. And rehearsal is not always about imagining yourself playing perfectly.

Boston Celtics player Kyrie Irving prepares mentally by thinking about his opponent's tendencies or tactics before the game. He also imagines or rehearses shooting game-winning shots or moves he will use in big moments of the game. Rehearsing yourself performing well in the game helps give you the confidence you can do it.

OTHER CONFIDENCE BOOSTERS

1. Be Prepared for Anything. Unexpected things happen during games that can hurt your composure and confidence. You want to be prepared to cope with adversity if and when it happens. You prepare your mind by anticipating as many challenges as possible. Challenges might include the gym is too hot, hostile crowd, taunting by opponents, bad calls from referees, not having your A-game, having a slow start on offense, etc.

Thus, you want to be prepared for situations in which you get upset, frustrated, or lose confidence during a game. For example, how will you react if you commit a bad foul? How will you let go of this and move on to the next play? You might prepare a Three Rs for coping with making a bad foul. Recognize you're dwelling on the foul. Regroup and interrupt that line of thinking. Finally, refocus on the current possession.

2. Let go of strict expectations. Expectations about your performance can hurt confidence when you think you're not performing up to your expectations. You learned about how to replace your expectations with process goals or objectives in Workbook 1.

3. Be More Accepting of Your Performance. When you judge how well you're performing during a game, this hurts your confidence and composure. You can't expect to have your A-game every time you play. If you are critical or judgmental during games, this means you have high expectations: "How am I performing compared to what I expect of myself?" Remember, the key is to not judge your performance during play—save it for after the game. Remind yourself to move on to the next play or possession.

4. Ride the changes in momentum. Momentum is a form of confidence. Sometimes you have momentum during a game—when your team goes on a run—and other times you don't have momentum. Instead of thinking "I've lost confidence in my shot," think about starting the momentum or gaining it back. Remember, you are still the same ball player with the same skills—at the moment you are not "hot" and that's part of playing the game.

5. Add your sources of confidence in your performance routine. See pages 3 and 4 of this workbook. What sources could you control? Add those sources to your performance routine. For example, studying the scouting report the day of the game, having a healthy meal, and practicing shots in shoot around that you will take during the game. Incorporate your sources of confidence in your performance outline to maintain consistent proactive confidence.

SUMMARY

Today, you learned how to be proactive with confidence. Proactive confidence means powering up your confidence during your warm-up and not waiting until you make a good play. Take control of your confidence—don't leave it to luck. You get proactive confidence from recalling your confidence résumé, using powerful self-talk, rehearsing successful plays in your mind, and overcoming self-critical thinking that destroys confidence.

No one can make you feel confident, but yourself. Likewise, no one can make you doubt your ability but yourself! Confidence must start on the inside based on your abilities and talents that help you succeed. Focus on your talents and strengths, not your shortcomings! Do not allow circumstances outside of your control, such as poor calls by officials, opponents taunting, or what others say to influence your confidence level.

THIS WEEK'S ACTION PLANS

Please apply the mental strategies you learned this week to practice, scrimmages, and games using the action plans below.

1. Awareness Exercise

Add to your confidence résumé as often as you think of new skills, strengths, or positive experiences to include. Make note of your thoughts and self-talk when you are performing well. Ask others to help you expand your confidence résumé.

2. Practice Plan

Begin to memorize your confidence résumé by rehearsing it prior to practice. Integrate your self-talk into your performance during practice. Begin to work on your mental rehearsal prior to practice.

3. Game-Time Application

Review your confidence résumé prior to a game. Think about having stable confidence during games no matter how well you're performing. Use your positive self-talk to help you stay confident. Use your mental rehearsal to experience yourself performing well in the game and coping well with adversity.

POST-GAME ASSESSMENT FOR CHAPTER 3

After your next scrimmage or game, please answer a few questions about your mental game. It's best if you answer them on the same day as your scrimmage or game. After you answer the questions below, reflect on how you can do better with proactive confidence.

1. What are two things you did well today as far as your mental game and performance?

2. What are two things you would like to improve for the next practice or game?

3. How would you rate your confidence (1-10) going into today's game? How stable was your confidence today?

4. Did you remain confident after a poor warm up or tough start to the game?

5. What did you do to feel confident before today's game?

6. What hurt your confidence, such as doubt, before or during the game?

7. Based on your answers to the questions here, what aspect of your mental game do you want to improve for your next practice or game?

MY NOTES

MY NOTES

MY NOTES

MY NOTES

CHAPTER 4

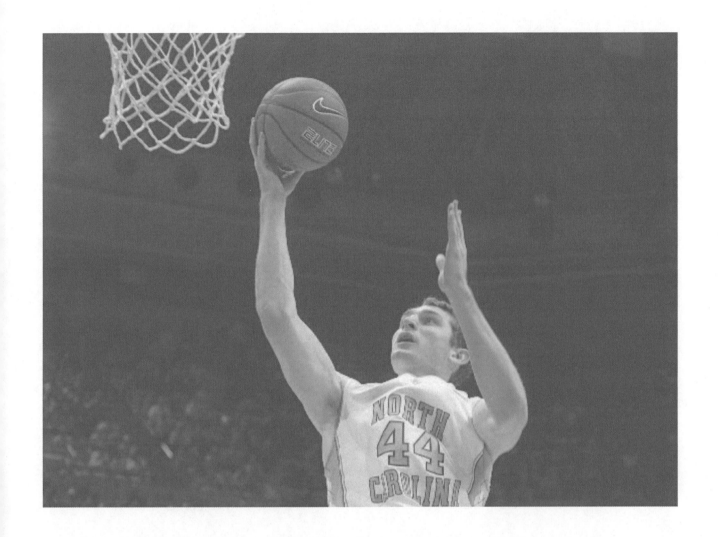

BUILD SELF-CONFIDENCE

HOW TO MANAGE CONFIDENCE-KILLERS

CHAPTER 4 OBJECTIVE

To learn how to overcome the most common confidence killers for you so you can have stable self-confidence.

WHAT YOU NEED TO KNOW

You've learned from Workbook 3A that stable, proactive confidence is important to your game. Likewise, it's important to know what hurts your confidence and how to overcome your personal confidence-killers, such as self-doubt or making comparisons to others.

> "Be aware of what hurts your confidence and how to overcome the confidence-killers"

When you have doubt, negative self-talk, or make comparisons to other athletes, your confidence will be fragile or unstable.

KEY POINT: To have high, stable confidence, you'll need to manage and overcome each confidence killer.

COMMON CONFIDENCE KILLERS

In your workbook, you will see a list of the most common confidence killers for athletes. This is not a complete list, but the most common ones. Let's see which ones apply to you.

EXERCISE 1: WHAT ARE YOUR CONFIDENCE KILLERS?

What hurts your confidence? Please place a check next to the statements that apply to you. You can also write down any others that aren't listed.

Common Confidence Killers	✓
1. **Having strict expectations.** Do you have strict expectations and lose confidence when you don't meet them?	
2. **Having self-doubt.** Do you question your ability to perform, such as "Will my shot be good today?"	
3. **Poor preparation.** Do you question the quality of your preparation or practice	
4. **Making comparisons to other athletes.** Do you compare yourself to other athletes or to the opposing team?	
5. **Worrying about what others think of your game.** Do you make assumptions that others think you're not a good athlete and this must be true?	
6. **Perfectionism or the need to be perfect.** Do you think you have to perform perfectly all the time or make no mistakes?	
7. **Lack of trust in your skills during games.** Do you feel like you don't trust your moves in games, play it safe, or perform too tentatively compared to practice?	
8. **Focusing on mistakes or mishaps.** Do you dwell on mistakes or mishaps during games and allow this to hurt your confidence or play too safe?	
9. **Having a poor pregame warm-up.** Do you lose confidence if you didn't have a good pregame warm-up?	
10. **Being self-critical after games.** Do you judge your game every play or are self- critical of mistakes you made after each game?	
What else hurts your confidence?	

MANAGING THE CONFIDENCE KILLERS

Let's examine these 10 confidence-killers and how you can manage each one better. You'll want to work on the confidence-killers that are relevant to you.

1. STRICT EXPECTATIONS

In Workbook 1, you learned about the confidence-expectation connection. Having high expectations can undermine your confidence when you feel you're not performing up to these expectations. The most important lesson you learned is to be aware of when you have these expectations and discard them. The goal is to replace your expectations with smaller, more manageable objectives prior to games.

> "Having high expectations can undermine your confidence."

Please review Workbook 1 for more information about managing expectations that undermine your confidence.

2. OVERCOMING SELF-DOUBT

The strongest confidence killer is self-doubt. When you doubt or question your ability, it's much harder to perform with confidence and trust in your skills. The goal is to rebut or reframe doubts quickly, so they don't hurt your confidence.

What Doubts Do You Have?

Most athletes will notice two kinds of doubt: (1) direct and (2) subtle. For example, a direct doubt is when you think, "My shot is off today, I can't make a basket today! I should stop shooting." An example of a subtle doubt is, "I wonder if my shot will show up today?"

KEY POINT: Anytime you question your skills, this is a doubt in disguise!

Common things you might have self-doubt about:

1. How your performance feels to you: "My shot doesn't feel good today. I'm unsure about my ability to make shots."

2. Your level of physical preparation: *"Am I strong enough to guard my opponent? Do I have enough stamina to finish the game strong?"*

3. How you feel about your recent practice: *"I haven't been having good practices lately, I'm wasting them and not improving."*

4. The strength of your mental game: *"I don't think I can handle the pressure."*

5. Your fitness level going into games: *"Am I fit enough to go four quarters?"*

6. How others think you can perform: *"I don't think my teammates like my game."*

7. How you stack up to the other team: *"We're going to get crushed by this team."*

8. Your ability to perform: *"Can I do a good job today for my teammates?"*

9. Your ability to perform well after an injury: *"Will I be able to perform up to the same level before this injury happened?"*

10. Past performances that haunt you: *"I played poorly against this team the last time. Will it happen again?"*

EXERCISE 2: CHALLENGE YOUR SELF-DOUBT

You want to rebut your self-doubt. There are two steps in the process:

1. Write down each doubt—as if you're thinking aloud: "I don't have my shot today."
2. Refute or challenge each doubt: "I can hit my shots like I do every game. Trust my shot and keep shooting."

In the table below, write the most common doubts that you have before or during a game in the left column. Next, refute or rebut each doubt similar to the example above. Be sure to memorize your rebuttal to each doubt so you can use them in games.

Table on the next page...

Challenge Your Self-Doubt

Top 5 Common Doubts	Refute Statement
1.	1.
2.	2.
3.	3.
4.	4.
5.	5.

3. QUESTIONING YOUR PREPARATION

Do you doubt the quality of your practice and training in the days leading up to a game and feel unprepared? Perfectionist athletes don't feel fully prepared when practice was not productive or perfect.

For example, do you feel as if "the stars have to align" to think you can perform well in the game? Great athletes are able to stay confident even when the starts don't align.

EXERCISE 3: HOW TO FEEL PREPARED

In the space provided below, what five reasons that you feel prepared? You might think about your preparation, putting in extra reps, feeling fresh, knowing the scouting report or the fact you are improving your mental game. Focus on what makes you feel prepared to play instead of what might be missing in your preparation.

1. ______________________________

2. ______________________________

3. ______________________________

4. ______________________________

5. ______________________________

Remember, stable confidence comes from years of practice and play, belief in your skills, and past experience. Even if you didn't have a perfect preparation, rely on years of practice and experience to feel prepared and confident.

"Stable Confidence comes from years of practice and play..."

4. COMPARING YOURSELF TO OTHER ATHLETES

Do you make comparisons to other athletes who you think are better? Do you look for other athletes who might be doing better or have better skills than you? Focusing on others' talents or success hurts your confidence when you think others are better than you.

EXERCISE 4: WHAT COMPARISONS DO YOU MAKE?

First, who do you compare yourself to, and second, what comparisons do you make? For example, you might make comparisons about physical prowess, size, speed, statistics, past results, or mental game strength.

What Comparisons Do You Make?

Who Do You Compare Yourself To?	What Comparisons Do You Make?
1.	1.
2.	2.
3.	3.
4.	4.
5.	5.

Your goal is to stop making comparisons to others. Start by recognizing when you're focusing on others' talents. Next, focus on your unique talents, skills, or strengths, such as your quickness, strength, technique, or being a leader. Choose the top five strengths from your confidence résumé, such as your abilities, strengths, speed, or strategy. Write those strengths below:

My Top Strengths:

1. ______________________________

2. ______________________________

3. ______________________________

4. ______________________________

5. ______________________________

Start during the warm-up. Put on your "imaginary blinders" to only focus on yourself and your team's warm-up routine. If you notice you're making comparisons, stop and think only about your pregame warm-up routine (review Workbook 2 on refocusing).

5. WORRYING ABOUT WHAT OTHERS THINK

Mind reading or thinking about what others MIGHT think about you, can hurt your confidence, especially when you assume that others think you're not doing well. Mind reading makes you project your thoughts onto others and think it must be true. However, you don't really know what others think about your game—you can only guess based on your own beliefs and perceptions.

First, you want to be aware when you mind read. Second, you have to challenge your mind reading. You do this by looking at the facts—a reality check if you will. For example, how do you know for a fact that others think this way? Where is the evidence others think this way? You don't really know unless you get practical evidence, such as if you ask others what they think, or they say something to you about your game.

EXERCISE 5: WHAT ASSUMPTIONS DO YOU MAKE?

In the space provided below, write down what you assume others think of your game and when you mind read, such as "I assume others think I can't shoot after I miss two shots in a row."

1. ______________________________

2. ______________________________

3. ______________________________

4. ______________________________

5. ______________________________

You want to separate fact from fiction when you assume others think you're not performing well. What do you know for a fact about these assumptions? Test out each one of your assumptions in reality. Where is the evidence that others actually think this way?

Lastly, catch yourself in the act of mind reading and refocus on what you're doing in the moment.

6. PERFECTIONISM OR THE NEED TO BE PERFECT

Perfectionism is a big confidence killer when you expect you'll perform perfectly every game or play. In addition, if you think "the stars have to align" to perform well on game day, this can hurt your confidence when you think something is not right.

EXERCISE 6: PERFORM FUNCTIONALLY, NOT PERFECTLY

The goal should not be to look, feel, or perform perfectly. Playing perfectly is not a good goal. The team with the most points wins. Trying to avoid mistakes, playing tentatively, and losing confidence after mistakes are the trap of perfectionists. How can you have a functional mindset during games?

Here is some self-talk to help you with this:

- "My performance doesn't have to look and feel good all the time to help my team."
- "My objective is to help my team score and play good D, not be perfect."
- "Mistakes are part of the playing the game and I accept that."
- "I'll get the job done even when I don't have my A-game."
- "The stars do not have to align to perform well."

Your Functional Mindset

What self-talk can you use to help you perform functionally in stead to trying to be perfect?

1. ______________________________

2. ______________________________

3. ______________________________

4. ______________________________

5. ______________________________

Helping your team win games is the goal. Stop judging your performance in every possession.

7. LACK OF TRUST IN YOUR SKILLS IN GAMES

Lack of trust in your skills also can hurt confidence. When you fail to trust your skills, you can't perform your best. Underperforming in games can hurt your confidence when you know you played tight or afraid to make mistakes.

> "Every time I rise up, I have confidence that I'm going to make it."
>
> — Stephen Curry

Several things affect trust in your skills including fear of failure, social approval, and anxiety about your performance. Many other mental skills have to fall in place for you to fully trust in your skills, including:

1. Managing the need to be perfect.

2. Transitioning from the training mindset into trust mode.

3. Overcoming fear of failure.

4. Stop worrying about what others think.

5. Improving your trust in skills by simplifying your performance.

This topic is covered fully in Workbook 4 where you'll learn more about what blocks your trust and what changes to make to improve trust in your skills.

8. FOCUSING ON MISTAKES OR MISHAPS

If you constantly dwell on your mistakes, you'll feel less confident. Thinking about past mistakes and how to not make more mistakes leads to performing tentatively or safe during games. If you miss your shots early in the game, do you stop shooting and instead pass the ball? It's part of the perfectionist mindset.

The key is to not dwell on mistakes, so they don't hurt confidence. This means moving on to the next play, without thinking about the last one. First, you want to accept that mistakes are part of the sport. Second, you have to quickly MOVE ON to the next play after making a mistake. This is a lesson you'll learn in Workbook 5.

EXERCISE 8: MOVING ON AFTER MISTAKES

List the common mistakes you dwell on in the left column. Write a corresponding statement to help you focus on "NEXT" shot or play. **For example, you might say:**

- "Move on, that's over."
- "I can't change the past. Next play!"
- "The past is the past. Get on with it."
- "Let's go—next play!"
- "Get your mind in the game."

Move On Statements

Mistakes	Move On
Missing a free throw.	*"I'm not perfect. Focus on my next play only."*
1.	1.
2.	2.
3.	3.
4.	4.

9. JUDGING YOUR PREGAME WARM UP

Does a poor pregame warm-up cause you to doubt your skills before tip-off? When you base your confidence on how the warm-up feels or how you performed in the warm-up, your confidence suffers—especially when you think the warm-up wasn't good.

You don't want to judge how well you did or feel during the warm-up. The warm-up is just a warm-up and you don't have to win the warm-up. Pregame is a time to transition into trusting mode and get your game face on.

You can use the following self-talk to help you stay confident in the warm-up:

- "I don't have to win the warm-up. It's just a warm-up."
- "My intensity will kick in and I'll focus better when the game starts."
- "My warm-up performance has nothing to do with how I'll do in the game."
- "I'll be ready to play when the game starts."
- "I've had great games in the past with a sub-par warm up.

10. BEING OVERLY CRITICAL POST-PERFORMANCE

How do you think about your performance after the game? Do you only focus on mistakes and missed shots? Do you focus on sub-standard stats? If you do this, you'll have a hard time growing your confidence from game to game because you think mostly about what you're doing wrong.

First, you want to focus on what you did well after every game. Second, you want to use every game to help you learn and improve your performance. This means assessing your performance and what you can work on in the next week of practice.

Post-Game Routine for Better Confidence

1. First, think about or review your best plays of your game. You might rehearse these in your mind.

2. Next, assess your performance objectively and decide what you want to improve during the next week of practice.

3. Leave the basketball on the court when you leave.

4. Switch roles and transition into other parts of your life.

SUMMARY

Confidence comes from the belief in your abilities and talents, which can help you succeed. Focus on what you do well, not your shortcomings! Do not allow the confidence-killers, such as having a poor warm-up or focusing on mistakes influence your confidence level.

First, you have to be aware of what hurts your confidence. Second, you have to work to negate the confidence killers that undermine your confidence. High expectations and self-doubt are the biggest confidence killers for athletes. To have stable confidence, you have to get off the confidence roller-coaster.

THIS WEEK'S ACTION PLANS

Please apply the mental strategies you learned this week to practice and games using the action plans below.

1. Awareness Exercise

Keep track of your negative thoughts or doubts about your ability and record these after each game. You want to practice reframing these doubts before the next game.

2. Practice Plan

Practice using your rebuttals to reframe the doubts you recorded after the game. List each doubt and your specific rebuttals for each. Rehearse these rebuttals in your mind to help you memorize them. The next level is to visualize or mentally rehearse rebutting doubts in practice.

3. Game-Time Application

Accept your warm-up for what it is—just a warm-up. Focus on stable confidence during pregame no matter how many mistakes you make. Let go of any outcome expectations you have about your stats or game performance. Also, put your doubt rebuttals and self-talk into the game.

POST-GAME ASSESSMENT FOR CHAPTER 4

After your next scrimmage or game, please answer a few questions about your mental game. It's best if you answer them on the same day as your scrimmage or game. After you answer the questions below, reflect on how you to overcome confidence killers.

1. What are two things you did well today as far as your mental game and performance?

2. What are two things you would like to improve for the next game?

3. Did you lose any confidence after your warm-up?

4. What pregame doubts did you have, if any?

5. What did you do to feel confident before your game today?

6. What other confidence-killers did you notice before or during today's game?

7. Based on your answers here, how can you feel more confident in the next game by managing the confidence killers?

MY NOTES

MY NOTES

MY NOTES

MY NOTES

CHAPTER 5

TRUST IN YOUR SKILLS

OVERCOME FEAR OF FAILURE & EXTEND PRACTICE PERFORMANCE TO GAMES

CHAPTER 5 OBJECTIVE

To understand the difference between a practice mindset and a performance mindset for games and to trust in your skills during games.

WHAT YOU NEED TO KNOW

You must embrace two different mindsets to reach your full potential as an athlete. These are: (1) The practice mindset and (2) the performance or game-time mindset. The practice mindset helps you improve your skills for future games. With a practice mindset, you focus on improving your skills, technique, and tactics. Here, you improve your skills today to play better in the next game.

> "You must embrace two different mindsets to reach your full potential as an athlete"

Alternatively, the game-time mindset (or trust mindset) helps you perform athletically in games. Here, you rely on the skills you trained in practice. The objective is to perform freely and intuitively, thus playing on instinct. When performing in games, you don't want to overthink or self-coach, such as, "use correct footwork, square up, bend elbow, follow through to the target, etc." In other words, the game-time mindset helps you trust in your learned skills. You want to get into the flow of the game and play athletically.

Don't confuse "trust in your skills" with confidence. However, when you have high confidence, it's easier to trust in your skills. Having high confidence allows you to let it happen or react intuitively during games.

Confidence is a belief in your ability to execute your skills. "I believe I can make this shot." Trust in your skills is getting into the flow of the game and playing athletically by "reacting to what you see, letting it happen, and getting the job done."

PRACTICE MINDSET VS. PERFORMANCE MINDSET

Both mindsets are important, but at the right time: (1) The practice mindset help you improve your game in practice and workouts and (2) The performance mindset helps you play athletically and intuitively during games. Most dedicated athletes are very good with the practice mindset but can overthink their performance during games.

Practice and Performance Mindset

Practice Mindset	Performance Mindset
▪ Good for practices	▪ Good for games
▪ Cognitive control of movements	▪ Automatic execution of skills
▪ Active mind	▪ Passive mind
▪ Inquisitive thinking	▪ Quiet mind
▪ Evaluate	▪ Performance mindset
▪ Judgmental	▪ Non-judgmental
▪ Critical of self	▪ Acceptance
▪ Force it to happen	▪ Letting it happen
▪ Over analysis	▪ Respond to the play
▪ Impatience	▪ Patience
▪ Work on technique	▪ Play the game
▪ Need to look good	▪ Just get the job done
▪ Strive for expectations	▪ Throw away expectations
▪ Focus on improvement for future	▪ Present orientation
▪ Rely on technique	▪ Rely on instincts

HOW DO ATHLETES DESCRIBE TRUST?

What does it feel like when you have full trust in your skills? Here's the way that athletes describe playing with trust:

1. "I was in the zone or flow."

2. "My performance felt effortless."

3. "I was just letting it happen."

4. "I felt as if I was on autopilot."

5. "I relied on what I've practiced."

6. "I felt relaxed and in the flow."

7. "I only reacted and didn't think."

8. "I was really locked in and decisive."

EXERCISE 1: WHAT'S IT LIKE WHEN YOU PERFORM WITH TRUST?

Describe your performance when you are playing with trust and your skills flow.

1. ____________________

2. ____________________

3. ____________________

4. ____________________

5. ____________________

STEP 1: WHAT ARE YOUR TRUST BREAKDOWNS?

To understand the idea of trust better, it helps to understand what hurts your ability to trust in your skills. I call these breakdowns in trust. Below are seven ways that hurt the ability to trust in your skills.

EXERCISE 2: WHAT ARE YOUR TRUST BREAKDOWNS?

What trust breakdowns do you identify with? Place a check mark next to the trust breakdowns you agree with:

Trust Breakdowns

Breakdown	Description	✓
1. Being too technical with your skills	Thinking too much about your technique. Stuck in the practice mindset during games.	
2. Over controlling your skills	Trying too hard to perform well. Steering, guiding, or over thinking your shot; trying too hard to be precise.	
3. Indecisive with or without the ball	Being unsure about what the best option is and hesitating.	
4. Perfectionism	Trying too hard to be perfect with your performance.	
5. . Over-analysis	Analyzing mistakes and fixing your technique during a game.	
6. Lack of confidence	Lack full confidence in your skills	
7. Fear of failure, tension or anxiety	Thinking about outcomes, losing, or disappointing others or feeling anxious, tense, or fearful in the game.	

Pressure and worry cause most athletes to tighten up and lose trust. Using the list above as a guide, think about the most common ways that you lose trust in your skills during games. Understanding what hurts your trust can help you change your approach to games and perform more athletically.

STEP 2: HOW DOES YOUR PERFORMANCE CHANGE?

Next, when you're not fully trusting in your skills, how does this change your performance? Here, you want specific situations (i.e. missing shots) that hurt your trust in your skills.

Here are some examples of how your performance might change when you lose trust:

- You become afraid of making mistakes and thus play it safe.
- You perform tentatively, not wanting to mess up.
- You stop taking risks or going for it.
- You're stuck in or revert back to a practice mindset.
- You over-analyze mistakes and try too hard to adjust.
- You try too hard to make up for previous mistakes.
- You're having a great game and worry about messing up.
- Your team is leading a close game and you don't want to mess up.

EXERCISE 3: SPECIFIC SITUATIONS WHEN YOU LOSE TRUST

If you are unsure about how to complete this exercise, you can complete it over the next few days of practice or after the next game as you think about what hurts your trust.

Missing Shots Early in the Game:

- Trigger or situation: "I missed two shots early in the game."
- What's the trust breakdown? "I became indecisive about shooting."
- How does performance change? "I stopped shooting and passed more."

"Once you've done the mental work, there comes a point where you have to throw yourself into the action and put your heart on the line."

— Phil Jackson

Keep in mind that lack of trust is not always about game situations, such as missing shots early in the game. For example, you might enter the game being scared to disappoint your teammates or coach, get tight, or not trust your decisions from the start.

What are the triggers, thinking patterns, or situations that lead to trust breakdowns? In the following table, please list specific situations (or thinking patterns) that undermine trust, the trust breakdown, and how your game changed.

Situations You Lose Trust

Situation	Trust Breakdown	Performance Change
1.		
2.		
3.		
4.		
5.		

HOW TO IMPROVE GAME-TIME TRUST

Here are four mental game strategies you'll want to master to improve trust when performing:

1. Be decisive when making decisions during games.

2. Keep your thinking simple by playing athletically.

3. Use the skills you have that day.

4. Stay in the moment and don't think ahead.

> "When you are indecisive about what to do on and off the ball, this leads to a breakdown in your trust and hesitation"

Let's examine each of these strategies...

(1) Be Decisive in Games

You want to play decisively in games. When you are indecisive about what to do on and off the ball, when shooting, or what defense to run, this leads to a breakdown in your trust and hesitation.

What thinking (or over thinking) might cause you to be indecisive during games? Below are a few examples:

1. Indecision with what play the team is running.

2. Unsure whether to dribble, pass or shoot.

3. Unsure who to guard on defense or what defense you're playing.

4. Second-guessing if you should take the shot.

5. Unsure what coach wants you to do.

6. Unsure about your off-ball movements or position on the court.

EXERCISE 4: BE 100% DECISIVE

Are you indecisive with the ball or off the ball? Review the chart in Exercise 3. How will you be more decisive in the game? What can help you commit to the plan or play?

Here's an example:

- **Problem:** You second-guess what to do when you have the ball – shoot, drive, or pass.
- **Be decisive:** Fully commit to the intuitive play that comes to mind. Go with your first instinct—trust your basketball instincts.

What's your plan for being more decisive on every play?

1. ______________________________

2. ______________________________

3. ______________________________

4. ______________________________

5. ______________________________

KEY POINT: How can you be more decisive and not second-guess your decisions? You want to rely on your practice and training and know intuitively what to do in that moment.

Here's how to play more decisively:

- Go with your first instinct when making split-second decisions (the first plan that comes to mind).
- Trust your basketball "instincts" (years of practice) to make the right decision.
- Mentally rehearse performing decisively before games.
- Think less about the right play and react based on what you see.

(2) How To Simplify Your Game

Simplifying your game means quieting the mind and not over-coaching yourself. A noisy mind may sound like this: "Oh my gosh, what's the play, I hope I don't mess up, don't make a turnover, my shoe is untied, my teammates depend on me... Will my coach be happy?" A quiet mind sounds more like this: "See the court and trust my basketball instincts."

EXERCISE 5: SIMPLIFY YOUR GAME

How do you keep it simple during games? You don't want to make playing the game more complex than need be. You simplify by parking the practice mindset so you can get into the flow of the game. Here are some examples of what you can do to quiet your mind:

1. Focus on one performance cue at a time (review workbook 2), such as court awareness.

2. Focus on one or two process goals for offense and defense, such as be decisive on the ball and play aggressive on defense.
3. Avoid judging how well you are doing on every possession. Just move on to the next play.
4. Stop analyzing and trying to fix your game, which may not be broken.

Pick one skill based on your position. What do you think about when you play effortlessly or with flow? Write your answer below. Here's an example to help you get started:

- **Shooting a Jump shot:** I just think about the back of the rim, the height of the shot, or visualize the trajectory of the shot.

Your coach (or mental coach) can help you simplify your game. Pick one skill (shooting, dribbling, passing, or other and describe what it's like when playing simple basketball:

1. ______________________________

2. ______________________________

3. ______________________________

4. ______________________________

3. Use the Skills You Have Today

Top ball players—who are gamers—can transition out of the practice mindset when they perform in the game. They trust all the work and preparation they have done leading up to the game. Instead of trying to improve for the future, you want to use what skills you have that day, which may not be perfect.

Remind yourself that you've put in all the work needed to perform well in the game. Commit to letting go of the practice mindset and think about playing great no matter if you have your A-game, B-game, or C-game!

4. Stay in the Moment

In this workbook, you've learned that thinking ahead about outcomes, stats, or what others might think about your performance leads to a trust breakdown because you start to play tight or afraid to mess up.

To fully trust in your skills and play athletically, you have to keep your mind on the moment-by-moment action of the game. We call this getting immersed into the flow of the game.

If you notice that you are thinking ahead about needing to score on a possession or worrying if others are going to be happy with your performance, stop and remind yourself to stay in the present moment—one play at a time. Treat each play as a game within itself. You can't play intuitively if you're worried about outcomes or your performance.

WARM-UP KEYS FOR GAME-TIME TRUST

Remember, the warmup is not a practice session or time to judge your game. The warm-up is just a warm up. The warm-up helps you transition from the practice mindset to the performance mindset. Please use the self-talk below when you start your warm-up:

Use this self-talk during the warm up:

1. "All my practice is complete. Now is the time to use my skills in the game."
2. "I don't have to win warm-ups. It's just a time to get ready and get into the flow."
3. "I'm prepared to use my skills I have today. The warm up is not a practice."
4. "No matter how my warm-up feels, I can get the job done in the game. Once the game starts, I'll be ready to go."

PRACTICE KEYS FOR IMPROVING GAME-TIME TRUST

How can you change how you practice so that you can improve trust during games? The objective is to divide practice into two objectives. First, practice is to improve your skills. Use one-half of practice to improve basic skills.

The second objective of practice is to learn to trust your skills or apply the game-time mindset. You should work on the trust mindset during scrimmages. Here, you want to "test" what you have been practicing by performing as if you were in a game—on autopilot or instinctively.

Simulation practice is a good way to work on trusting your skills. Here, you might imagine a pressure situation you'll encounter in games. For example, you might pretend you are in the last two minutes of a tied game and you fully trust in your ability to make a shot.

Strategies to Increase Trust During Practice

1. Taper off the practice mindset as you get closer to game day. Work less on skills or form and more on playing intuitively in the flow.
2. Think less and react more during part of your practice. Let go of overthinking and use your basketball instincts.
3. Use the 50/50 rule during practice: trust your skills 50% of the time during practice.
4. Imagine performing well in game situations. Visualize yourself playing with high trust and flow.

KEY POINT: Most importantly, you want to adopt a game-time mindset during practice. This way you can trust your skills more readily during games.

BECOME A GAMER

One quality of top athletes is the ability to get the job done when they don't have their A-game. You will not have your A-game every day for many different reasons. This is when you need to perform functionally and not fret about how well you are performing. A "functional mindset" is called being a "gamer." This means you stay mentally tough and fight until the last second of the game, even when you don't feel at your best or have made a few mistakes.

A functional mindset means getting the job done—helping your team score or causing a turnover on defense without regard to looking or feeling correct. If you become frustrated or self-critical of your performance, it's hard to keep your head in the game. With a functional mindset, you accept imperfection, mistakes, and not feeling on. This is when being non-judgmental about your game is super important.

KEY POINT: A functional mindset is also about "winning ugly." Winning ugly is finding a way to get the job done no matter how it looks or feels to you.

Strategies for a Functional Mindset

1. Know that your practice is complete when you start a game. Stop practicing for the future and use your skills to get it done today.

2. Perform efficiently instead of perfectly. This means that sometimes you have to abandon the perfect or correct way to perform. Use whatever works to help you get the job done in games. Embrace the play that worked even though you didn't execute it perfectly.

3. Use what's working for you that day instead of trying to play "by the book." Stick to your "bread and butter" shot, for example. This is the shot that's working that day. Use what's working rather than getting bogged down in forcing plays you don't have.

4. Park your judgement or analysis during games. Avoid analyzing mistakes and trying to make technical adjustments during games. Over analysis of your mistakes only causes you to slip into the practice mindset. The best time to make corrections is after games or in your next practice.

SUMMARY

Trust in your skills by simplifying your performance and relying on motor memory (repetition) from practice. In games, you want to just "perform" and do what you already know. This means relying on your basketball instincts and allowing your skills to "just happen." Save practicing for the next practice. Avoid fixing, judging, or overanalyzing your game. For example, if you make a mistake, let it go and move on to the next play.

Trying to have the perfect performance should not be your goal. You can strive for perfection in practice but know you won't be in games. The obvious goal is to win, but today's most important lesson is to learn how to get through the game when you don't have your A-game. You are not always going to feel or look perfect on the court.

Be a "gamer" and perform the best you can on the day of the game. If you don't have your "A" game, then go to plan B. Embrace the fact that you might have to grind it out sometimes. Having to make the most of your skills doesn't mean the game will be a "bust." Use all the practice and preparation to trust in your ability to make it through the game.

THIS WEEKS ACTION PLANS

Please apply the mental strategies you learned this week to practice and games using the action plans below.

1. Awareness Exercise

Keep track of when and how your trust breaks down during practices and games. Record these after practice or games. You want to write down when the trust breakdown happened and what the trigger was. For example, missing shots leads to overthinking and tinkering with your technique.

2. Practice Plan

Avoid over training your technique. Stick to the 50/50 rule of training and trusting your skills. Taper off the amount of technical training you do in practice as you get closer to games.

3. Game-Time Application

Keep your performance simple in games. Trust your training and preparation to carry you through games. Remember, even when you don't have your "A" game, win ugly and play with the skills you have that day.

POST-GAME ASSESSMENT FOR CHAPTER 5

After your next scrimmage or game, please answer a few questions about your mental game. It's best if you answer them on the same day as your scrimmage or game.

1. What are two things you did well today with your mental game and performance?

2. What are two things you would like to improve for the next practice or game?

3. How functional was your performance and did you play with the skills you had today?

4. Did you make any assumptions about how you would perform based on the quality of your warm-up?

5. How much (%) of the game did you trust in your skills and get into the flow of the game?

6. How often did you lose trust in your game? Did you start the game with full trust in your skills?

7. Based on your answers to the questions here, what aspect of your mental game do you want to improve for your next practice or game?

MY NOTES

MY NOTES

MY NOTES

MY NOTES

CHAPTER 6

COMPOSURE

LEARN HOW TO RECOVER QUICKLY FROM MISTAKES

CHAPTER 5 OBJECTIVE

To learn how to let go of mistakes quickly so you can perform with composure and not compound mistakes.

WHAT YOU NEED TO KNOW

Mistakes happen in basketball. Mistakes can lead to frustration or anger, but it doesn't have to be this way. If your human, you will make mistakes every game. However, you want to learn to stay composed, so frustration or anger doesn't lead to more mistakes on the court. Letting go of mistakes is a skill that will help you overcome mishaps, mistakes, poor calls by officials, or any other challenge.

When frustrated about a mistake, your mind gets stuck in the past. This causes two problems: (1) you're frustrated and (2) lose focus in the moment. Your focus is split between thinking about the past mistake and trying to execute the next play. You can't perform well with a spilt focus or when dwelling on a mistake.

When you can let go of mistakes quickly, mistakes don't turn into more mistakes.

"When you can let go of mistakes quickly, they don't turn into more mistakes."

THE LOOK OF COMPOSURE

What does a composed athlete look like? What are the characteristics of composure? Please review the characteristics below:

- Head up, shoulders back
- Calm under pressure
- Not easily rattled
- Patient when trialing in a game
- Does not sulk or quit
- Accepts mistakes and moves on
- Relaxed disposition
- Moves on after mistakes without dwelling
- Strong finisher in crunch-time

EXERCISE 1: HOW DOES YOUR PERFORMANCE CHANGE?

How does your game change after making one or two mistakes? In the table below, check off all changes that apply to you. If one is not listed, please write it in the "other" space given.

How Your Performance Changes

Performance Change	✓
1. Speed up your game; play out of control, make rash decisions.	
2. Become frustrated, angry or upset.	
3. Lose focus as a result of dwelling on mistakes.	
4. Make more mental or physical errors.	
5. Lash out at teammates or opponents.	
6. Mental confusion or indecision	
7. Attempt to make up for mistakes and play overly aggressive.	
8. Challenge your opponents and get into foul trouble.	
9. Start to over play, such as make stronger passes or over play opponent on defense.	
Other changes:	

UNDERSTANDING COMPOSURE

Let's begin with four key concepts to help you understand composure:

1. **Frustration** – Being angry or upset about not reaching an expectation or goal.

2. **Dwelling** – Constantly thinking about something that is upsetting from the past, such as making a turnover, bad call by an official, or missing a shot.

3. **Expectation** – A standard you think you should achieve, such as, "I expect to not make mistakes, or I should score 10 points."

4. **Irrational Beliefs** – Unhealthy beliefs that can trigger your frustration, such as, "My teammates will be upset with me if I make too many mistakes."

In this lesson, you'll learn about how expectations and irrational thinking can lead you to being upset or frustrated.

THE FRUSTRATION SETUP

When you have rigid expectations, you're likely to become easily frustrated because you judge that you are not performing up to your expectations (see chapter 1). Thus, your expectations are often the root of the frustration setup.

EXERCISE 2: WHAT EXPECTATIONS CAUSE FRUSTRATION?

What expectations can trigger frustration when not met? For example, if you expect to always maintain possession of the ball, you might feel upset when you make a turnover. Please list five expectations that set up your frustration, such as, "I should never make a turnover."

Use your expectations from Workbook 1 to note which ones can trigger frustration:

1. ____

2. ____

3. ____

4. ____

5. ____

KEY POINT: Be sure to uncover the specific expectations that may hurt composure, discard them, and instead focus on small manageable objectives, such as making sharp passes or protect the ball on dribble (see chapter 1 for review).

YOUR REACTION TO MISTAKES

No one can make you feel frustrated with mistakes, but yourself! Just because you mess up doesn't mean you HAVE TO BE upset with yourself! This means that a mistake is only a trigger for you to react to—it doesn't mean you have to be upset. How you think about mistakes is the reason that you feel upset. Here's the model:

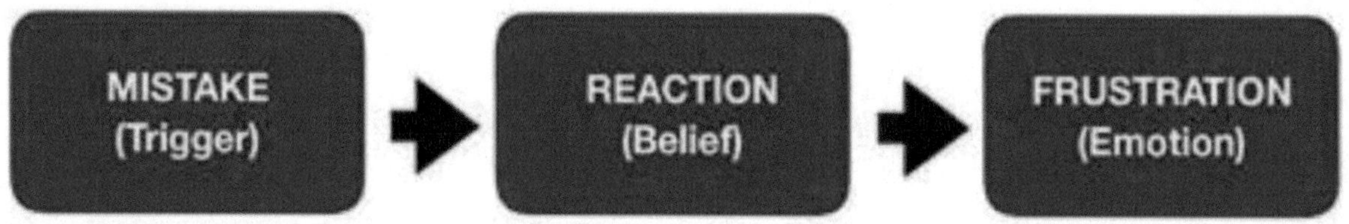

For example, if you miss an easy shot, do you have to feel frustrated? No, not really because missing a shot is simply a fact. Judging your performance harshly is the trigger for you to feel upset or frustrated. *You are in full control of how you react to mistakes!*

Thus, your reaction or thoughts about the missed shot is what causes you to become frustrated, not the mistake itself. That's right, mistakes don't cause you to be frustrated, you do!

Three Steps for Greater Composure:

1. Understand what mistakes (triggers) lead you to lose composure.

2. Realize how your beliefs (how you react to mistakes) lead you to feel frustrated.

3. Learning to think differently, react with composure, and not judge your performance after mistakes.

CHANGE YOUR RECTION TO MISTAKES

The goal is to learn how to change your reaction to mistakes so you can play on with a calm and composed mind.

Letting go of mistakes doesn't mean that you don't care. Rather, you realize dwelling on mistakes and getting upset won't change the past. Dwelling causes you to lose focus, perform tentatively, make bad decisions, and, in some cases, try too hard to make up for mistakes.

EXERCISE 3: TRIGGERS & HOW YOU REACT TO MISTAKES

The key to better composure is to change how you REACT to mistakes (triggers) and using your new reactions to change your emotion.

> "Everyone is going to make mistakes, but your energy and your effort makes up for those mistakes."
>
> — James Harden

Here is an example to help you get started:

- **Trigger:** Making a bad pass leading to a turnover.
- **Reaction:** *"I should never turn the ball over on a pass. That's unacceptable. My teammates hate me."*
- **Emotion:** Frustration about missing an opportunity to score.

Directions to Exercise 3: *Complete the three steps below for Exercise 3 using the table below:*

Step 1: In the left column, write down your top five triggers. These are the common mistakes or challenges (bad calls, taunting, etc.) that can trigger a negative reaction during the game.

Step 2: For each mistake or challenge, write down how you react to each trigger in the middle column below. This means how you think about each mistake or why it's upsetting to you, not the FACT you made a mistake.

Step 3: For each mistake or challenge, write down the emotion that follows the mistake in the right column. This might be feeling anger, frustration, surprise, helplessness, or fear of making more mistakes.

Table on next page...

Triggers and How You React to Mistakes

Trigger	Reaction	Emotion
1.		
2.		
3.		
4.		
5.		

EXERCISE 4: CHANGING YOUR REACTION TO MISTAKES

The most important step is to react differently to mistakes. You want to change the old reaction—that leads to frustration—to a new reaction, which helps you stay composed and focus on the next play. The objective is to forgive yourself or be okay with making a mistake. **To help you move on, you can combine two strategies:**

1. Rationalize with yourself to make the mistake okay.

- *"Even the pros make mistakes."*
- *"I'm not perfect."*
- *"Mistakes are part of sports."*
- *"My teammates understand because they make mistakes too."*
- *"The refs are not perfect. They make mistakes too."*
- *"No one can make me feel frustrated but myself."*

2. Refocus or "move-on" statements:

- *"Let it go, next play."*
- *"That's in the past, move on."*
- *"Finish strong."*
- *"I can recover."*

- *"The past is the past, I can only move*
- *on." "I'm in control. Get on with it."*
- *"I'm not perfect, no one is."*

"The goal is to stop thinking about the past mistake and get your mind on the next play."

For each trigger you listed in Exercise 2, copy them to the table below. In the right column, replace the old reaction to mistakes with a new reaction. The goal is to stop thinking about the past mistake and get your mind on the next play. Thus, you want to rationalize and recover to the next play.

Let's use the previous example:

- **Trigger:** You made a turnover.
- **Old Reaction:** "I should never turn the ball over on a pass. That's unacceptable. My teammates hate me right now."
- **New Reaction:** "I'm not perfect. Even the pros make turnovers. Let it go and focus on making accurate passes next time."

A New Reaction to Mistakes

Trigger	Old Reaction	New Reaction
1.		
2.		
3.		
4.		
5.		

CHAPTER 6 – COPING WITH MISTAKES

As an athlete and human, you will make mistakes—it's a part of sports. Certainly, you want to limit mistakes, but you have to accept and move on when they happen. It doesn't mean you shouldn't care about mistakes. Also, some triggers are outside of your direct control, such as bad calls from officials, fans in the stands, or attempts from your opponent to get into your head.

KEY POINT: You must not fret about the things that are beyond your control because you cannot change them.

ADDITIONAL TIPS FOR LETTING GO OF MISTAKES

1. Practice the 10-second rule after a mistake. Use a few seconds to process the mistake in your mind briefly. After 5-10 seconds, stop dwelling and move on to the next play. Hopefully, you can turn this into the 5-second rule and then the 2-second rule as you don't have much time between plays!

2. "Park" the mistake until after the game. You have no time to judge your play during the game. Park the mistake until after the game if you want to analyze any mistakes. Post-game is the time to objectively assess your performance and what you can improve in practice. Use your assessment of your game performance to improve performance in the next week of practice.

3. Use 4 get-out-of-jail-free cards during the game. Mistakes are part of the game. Avoid expecting a mistake-free game. Having no mistakes in a game sounds good, but not very practical for your composure. Give yourself 4 mistakes a game or get-out-of-jail cards. When you make a mistake, use one of your cards to forgive and forget. This helps you learn to move on quickly when they happen.

4. What would a positive coach or teammate tell you? It's hard to be objective with your performance during a game. One way to be more objective about how you react to mistakes is to step outside the emotion of the mistake. What would a positive coach or teammate tell you to help you move on,
such as, "Good try, don't worry, stuff happens."

5. Flush the mistake. Use a physical trigger as a symbolic gesture to letting go of the mistake... Swipe to the next page, flush the mistake down the toilet, or shoot the mistake into the trash.

6. Stop judging your performance. Having strict expectations for your performance causes you to judge your game every play. The more self-critical or judgmental you are, the harder it is to let go of mishaps. After a mistake or mishap, repeat to yourself: "NEXT...." Say next play, next possession, next shot, etc.

SUMMARY

When you become frustrated with mistakes, opponents, or officials, your mental game is thrown into disarray. Negative emotions lead to rushing, pressing, making mental errors, foul trouble, and inability to focus in the present. Keep in mind that mistakes are only triggers or facts and do not cause you to feel upset. How you react to mistakes or bad calls from officials is the reason you feel upset. The goal is to change how you think when you make mistakes and thus change your emotional reaction.

The important objective is to move past mistakes and setbacks quickly. As Ken Ravizza said many times, "It's very hard to play the game with a monkey on your back." You have to throw the monkey off your back. The sooner you can accept and let go of a mistake, the faster you can recover mentally and move on to the next play.

THIS WEEK'S ACTION PLANS

Please apply the mental strategies you learned this week to practice and games using the action plans below.

1. Awareness Exercise

After practice or the next game, be aware of the triggers that can lead to you feeling upset. After practice or the next game, record what the triggers were for your frustration, such as mistakes, refs, opponents, teammates, coaches, etc. And how did you think or react to each of these mistakes or challenges? For example, what did you say to yourself after the ref called you for a foul?

2. Practice Plan

Start by developing new reactions for each of your triggers. How will you react to reason and move on quickly? Memorize your new reactions. Better yet, practice your new way of responding to mistakes in your mind. Rehearse your new reactions at home and start to use them during practice.

3. Game-Time Application

Rehearse your new reactions to each trigger prior to the game. Use your new reactions to help you recover from mistakes during the game. After each game, note how successful you were in moving on after the mistake. Record on your mental game assessment for this chapter, the times when you were dwelling on a mistake or got stuck in frustration.

POST-GAME ASSESSMENT FOR CHAPTER 6

After your next scrimmage or game, please answer a few questions about your mental game. It's best if you answer them on the same day as your scrimmage or game.

1. What are two things you did well today with your mental game and performance?

2. What are two things you would like to improve for the next game?

3. How successful were you in letting go of mistakes or mishaps today? If you were not successful, what got in the way?

4. At what times during practice or competition did you get upset or frustrated with your game. List these and the corresponding frustration-provoking thoughts.

5. What thoughts helped you let go of mistakes that you can use in future competitions?

6. What did you learn about staying composed today that you can apply to future competitions?

7. Based on your answers to the questions here, what aspect of your mental game do you want to improve for your next scrimmage or game?

MY NOTES

MY NOTES

MY NOTES

MY NOTES

CHAPTER 7

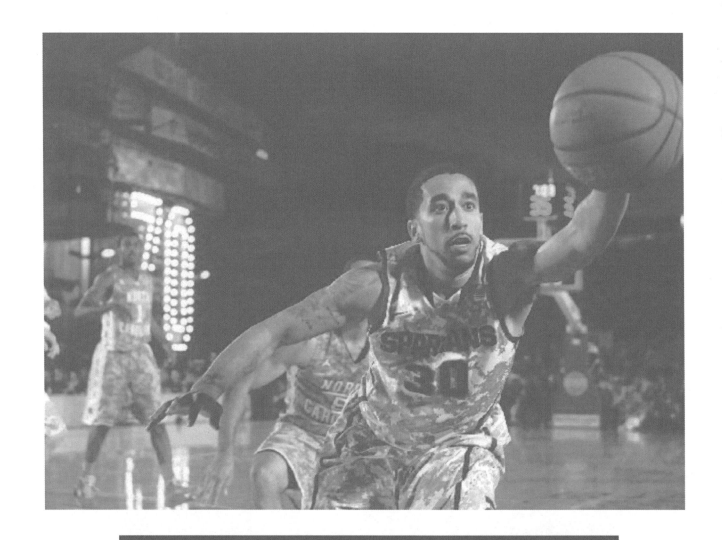

HOW TO OVERCOME FEAR OF FAILURE

LEARN HOW TO MOVE FORWARD DESPITE THE RISK OF FAILURE

CHAPTER 7 OBJECTIVE

You'll learn how to overcome fear of failure, so you can perform freely in games.

WHAT YOU NEED TO KNOW

Fear of failure causes most athletes to be anxious, which hurts their performance during games. When you feel anxious or tight, you perform tentatively and lack trust in your skills. Fear of failure often comes from the need for social approval or wanting to feel respected by teammates, coaches, fans, and parents. Fear of failure is very common among perfectionist athletes who want to perform well all the time.

Although anxiety and worry about your game performance seem very real to you, the supporting beliefs can be irrational, such as, "I must perform well today for others to respect me." All athletes want to perform well, but often times it's irrational to think that you *must* perform well for others to respect you. The biggest challenge with fear of failure is a lack of trust in your skills or performing cautiously.

> "The biggest challenge with fear of failure is a lack of trust in your skills or performing cautiously."

The most common fears associated with fear of failure:

- Fear of performing poorly.
- Fear of embarrassment.
- Fear of letting down teammates, coach, or parents.
- Fear of not performing up to one's potential.
- Fear of not meeting others' expectations.
- Fear of negative social evaluation.
- Fear of not being accepted or not gaining approval.
- Fear of sacrifice and not getting the "pay off."
- Fear of not being seen as the star of the team anymore.

Interestingly, the more you want to succeed in basketball, the harder you try to NOT fail and thus, the more tense or anxious you perform. This intense "wanting" to succeed causes you to focus more on avoiding mistakes and perform tentative in games. For example, missing a shot early in the game can cause you to play it safe.

EXERCISE 1: TEST YOUR FEAR OF FAILURE

Fear of failure does not come from external sources, such as playing a high-seeded opponent or a playoff game. It comes from your beliefs about needing to succeed or not failing. However, many fears are not rational not based in reality. Below is a table with common signs of fear of failure. Please mark all that apply to you.

Do You Have a Fear of Failure?

Common Signs of Fear of Failure	✓
1. You have difficulty taking your practice skills to games.	
2. You want to win or succeed badly, and this leads to playing cautiously.	
3. You focus too much on stats or outcomes and can't enjoy the process.	
4. You become impatient if you don't perform well in games.	
5. You often feel like your self-esteem is threatened when you do poorly.	
6. You care too much about what others think and assume what they think.	
7. You have a fear of letting others down if you don't perform well.	
8. You tighten up, freeze, or become tense in games and can't perform freely.	
9. You try too hard to win and get in your own way mentally with a lack of	
trust. 10. You badly want your hard work to "pay off" and not waste your time.	
11. Your pregame jitters turn into anxiety and stay after the start of games.	

If you checked off two or more of the statements in the table above, then fear of failure hurts your performance. If you agree with only one of the statements above, you will still benefit from learning more about fear of failure.

> "I have self-doubt. I have insecurity. I have fear of failure. I have nights when I show up at the arena and I'm like, 'My back hurts, my feet hurt, my knees hurt. I don't have it. I just want to chill.' We all have self-doubt. You don't deny it, but you also don't capitulate to it. You embrace it."
>
> — Kobe Bryant

Let's start with the underlying fear that holds you back, so you can address it head-on.

Fear of failure is often related to the following three areas:

1. Fear of working hard and sacrificing, but not getting the "payoff"

2. Fear of being rejected, losing respect, or embarrassment

3. Fear of not gaining others' approval, respect, or admiration

Numbers two and three above are the same challenge. What specific fear supports your fear of failure? Just knowing what causes your worry can help put you at ease. When you don't understand why you play cautiously, you can feel helpless. Once you understand the fear that holds back your game, you take its power away. In this chapter, you'll learn how to identify and overcome the fears discussed here.

EXERCISE 2. WHAT'S YOUR SPECIFIC FEAR?

Your fear might be straightforward: *"I'm worried that coach will bench me if I make mistakes."* But it's often not that easy, and you'll have to dig a bit to uncover the underlying fear. For example, you might feel anxious missing a free throw when trying to help your team win.

But the real fear might be that you don't want to disappoint your teammates or let down a coach. These fears are about what others might think if you don't perform up to their expectations. Hopefully, you're already closer to understanding the source of your underlying fear based on the examples presented earlier and the expectations you uncovered in chapter 1.

Please answer these important questions to discuss with your mental coach:

1. What's so awful for you if you have a bad game or don't perform well?

___

2. What's the worst thing that can happen if you lose or don't perform well?

___

3. Who do you think will be disappointed if you perform poorly, and why?

___

4. Whose respect or recognition do you want to gain via basketball, and why?

___

5. How would you feel if you gave up basketball due to not reaching your goals or injury?

___

The answers to these questions are not easy, but they should help you get closer to the underlying fears that hold you back. Keep in mind that your ultimate fear often relates to the need for social approval, which you've learned about in chapter 5.

HOW TO CONFRONT YOUR FEAR HEAD ON

Once you uncover the underlying fear, you're now in a position to confront your fear head-on. One of the ways you do this is by taking a new perspective about playing the game. This means having a healthier philosophy about playing basketball. For example, should your goal be to gain others' acceptance or enjoy playing the game? You'll also want to confront your fear using reason. If you're working with a mental coach, he or she can also help you determine what's rational and what's irrational about your fear.

STEP 1: CONFRONT YOUR FEAR

Start by uncovering the irrational beliefs that support your fears and replace those beliefs by taking a new perspective. Psychologist Dr. Albert Ellis would say that a belief or idea is irrational if:

- It distorts reality.
- It is illogical.
- It prevents you from reaching your goals.
- It leads to unhealthy emotions.
- It leads to self-defeating behavior.

STEP 2: BE RATIONAL ABOUT THE ROLE OF SPORTS IN LIFE

Ask yourself: *Does having this fear help me? What's a different way of looking at your fear?*

When you uncover the underlying fear, you want to challenge your beliefs about it. For example,

- *Will coach really bench you if you make a mistake?*
- *Will your teammates actually reject you if you make a turnover or miss a shot?*
- *Will you lose respect from others if you don't score the most points?*

Here are a few more suggestions to help you be more rational:

SEPARATE THE PERSON FROM THE ATHLETE

You've learned that fear of failure relates to social approval or the fear of not being respected by others, which can affect how you feel as a person. Consequently, your self-esteem is in jeopardy when you believe, **"***My self-worth (self-esteem) as a person depends on my success in sports***."**

What's the irrational belief here? It's thinking your self-worth comes from your achievement in basketball. Every time you have a bad game, your self-esteem takes a hit. You take it personally and attach failure in sports to your ego or self-esteem. If you think about poor performance for a few hours or more, that's a good sign you take it personally.

KEY POINT: You want to learn how to leave the basketball on the court and not take it home or feel upset for hours after a loss. You do this by successfully switching roles (student, son, daughter, friend, etc.) in your life when you get off the court.

STRIVE FOR GROWTH ORIENTATION

If you have a bad game, it doesn't mean YOU are a failure or a "loser." It only means that in one part of your life (basketball) and one day as an athlete, you did not perform up to expectations. So, your new perspective is: "I'm much more than how many points I score or how many mistakes I make on the court. I'm a good person no matter if I win or lose." "Basketball is something I choose I do, not who I am!"

Some athletes assume that failure is an end to playing basketball. They falsely assume they are not good enough to continue to play. The irrational belief is: "If I fail today, I'm done with basketball and others will not respect me." Failure is part of the process of learning and growing in sports. I'm sure when you first started playing basketball you had many setbacks that taught you valuable lessons—to help you grow as an athlete.

ADOPTING A NEW PERSPECTIVE ON SPORTS

Your new perspective is: "Failure is only temporary. It helps me learn, re-evaluate, and do something differently with new experiences." Having a new perspective doesn't happen overnight. It takes time to change old beliefs you've maintained for years.

> "Confidence helps you trust in the skills that you practice every day."

Do you feel others judge you if you don't perform up to their expectations? This is one of the core beliefs underlying fear of failure—the fear of how others might change their opinions of you if you don't perform up to their expectations. Dr. Ellis would say the irrational thinking here is: *"I must succeed and win the approval of others or else others will not view me as a worthy person."*

No matter how well you perform as an athlete, you're still the same person that people in your life appreciate. The people close to you won't change their opinions of you as a person! The people who matter most to you (e.g., true friends, family) will support you no matter what. Contrary to what you might think, others' opinions of you are not conditional on your success or failure in basketball. They support you unconditionally. Your new perspective is: "Others appreciate me for who I am no matter how successful I am in sports."

EXERCISE 3: MY NEW PERSPECTIVE IN SPORTS

In the table on the following page, write up to three or four irrational beliefs that support the fear(s) you uncovered in this workbook—in the left column. Write in the middle column, what's irrational about that belief—challenge the validity of your belief.

In the far right column, please state your new perspective or what we call a growth mindset. You'll see an example in the table to help you do this exercise.

My New Perspective in Sports

Your Belief	Irrational Part	Growth Mindset
"I need to be perfect and make zero mistakes today or others will be disappointed."	Thinking you have to be perfect for others to be happy with your game.	"Basketball is not a game of perfection. Accept I am human. Others respect me for who I am."
1.		
2.		
3.		
4.		

KEY POINT: Commit to changing how you think about basketball's role in your life. Embrace it as the best option to perform free of pressure. Remind yourself that you are still the same person others appreciate no matter how well you perform in sports.

DWELL IN POSSIBILITY

To further explore the concept of changing your perspective, consider this question to yourself: **"What if things go right?"** Have you ever thought of the potential scenario where everything goes exceptionally well, or even surpasses your highest expectations? The upcoming exercise aims to guide you in shifting your focus from problems to possibilities.

“I dwell in possibility.” -Emily Dickinson

Exercise 4: DWELL IN POSSIBILITY/ FLIP THE SCRIPT

Use the table on the next page to help you change the way you think from focusing on problems to thinking about possibilities. In this exercise, you'll write down a situation that makes you scared, then you'll write out the best thing that could happen in that situation. After that, you're asked to picture in your mind what the best-case scenario looks like. This helps your brain learn to think about good outcomes, not just bad ones. Doing this exercise is like teaching your brain a new way to think—instead of always expecting bad things, you'll start to get excited about all the good things that could happen.

DID YOU KNOW?: Visualizing a different outcome than the one you fear provides your subconscious with an alternative reality. You get to rewrite the script for a "what if" good instead of a "what if" bad. Visualizing best-case scenarios helps reduce fear and anxiety, boosts confidence, and aids in overcoming the fear of failure.

EXERCISE 4: DWELL IN POSSIBILITY / FLIP THE SCRIPT

Use the table below to help you shift your mindset from problems to possibilities. See the example in the table to assist you.

(1) In the left column write the problem or situation you are fearful of.
(2) Then in the right column write down the best-case scenario. Reflect on what it would look like if things go right. Think of a potential scenario where everything goes exceptionally well or even surpasses your highest expectations.
(3) After writing down the best-case scenario, take 5 minutes to visualize (picture yourself) experiencing that best-case scenario. Finally, put a check in the far right column once you completed the visualization exercise.

Dwell In Possibility/ Flip The Script

Fearful Situation	Best-Case Scenario	✓
Example: Making a lot of mistakes and embarrassing myself, coach, and parents.	**Example:** I recover quickly from my mistakes and score a career-high. We win the game and college coaches start reaching out to my coach about my performance.	✓

SUMMARY

Fear of failure will keep you stuck in a web of anxiety and tentative play if you don't uncover the underlying fear. In addition, you have to face the fear head-on. This means evaluating how irrational your fear really is and challenging it. For example, do you know for a fact that others change their opinion of you if you don't succeed or win?

The final and most important step for taking on your fears is to change your perspective or beliefs about sport. Create a "growth mindset" that will help you focus on success instead of fearing failure.

Psychologist Dr. Albert Ellis says that most people have a tendency to harbor irrational beliefs. He believed that unhelpful (or irrational) thinking creates unhealthy emotions and self-defeating behaviors. He taught people to change their irrational beliefs into realistic and helpful ones. Dr. Ellis called this process, "developing a more rational philosophy." Today you learned how this process works with the beliefs that support fear of failure.

THIS WEEK'S ACTION PLANS

Please apply the mental strategies you learned this week to practice and games using the action plans below.

1. Awareness Exercise

Be more aware of the signs of fear of failure listed in Exercise 1. What signs do you notice the most when you compete? How does your performance change when you experience these signs?

2. Practice Plan

Determine your ultimate fear or the fear underlying your fear of failure. Is your fear about what others might think of your performance? Or, if others will respect your skills? Or, are you worried about being rejected or embarrassed if you don't do well? Finally, is your fear about putting in all the work on not reaching your goals?

3. Game-Time Application

Put your new perspective into play. Remind yourself why you participate in sports. Play the game for yourself, not others. Focus on having a growth perspective and learning from mistakes. Understand that perfection is an ideal and not a good goal.

POST-GAME ASSESSMENT FOR CHAPTER 7

After your next scrimmage or game, please answer a few questions about your mental game. It's best if you answer them on the same day as your scrimmage or game.

1. What are two things you did well today with your mental game and performance?

2. What are two things you would like to improve for the next game?

3. How well did you perform fearlessly without tension or anxiety today?

4. How well did you focus on your new perspective of sports or play for yourself today? If this was hard to do, what made it difficult?

5. How well did you focus on what you want to do, instead of fearing what not to do?

6. How well did you let go of outcomes and consequences and enjoy yourself in the process or flow of the game?

7. Based on your answers to the above questions, what mental game skills would you like to improve before your next games?

MY NOTES

MY NOTES

MY NOTES

MY NOTES

CHAPTER 8

PREGAME MENTAL PREP

FOR PEAK PERFORMANCE

CHAPTER OBJECTIVE

You'll learn how to use your pregame routine to help you mentally prepare for each game.

WHAT YOU NEED TO KNOW

Your pregame warm up is the perfect time to get your game face on and prepare mentally for a game. The top three objectives of a pregame routine are to be focused, feel confident, and prepare to trust in your skills.

You can think of a pregame routine as an ideal time to apply the mental skills you've learned in this program to the game. You use a warm-up routine to get physically ready for the game. Here, you'll learn how to mentally prepare for a game.

When you have consistent mental preparation, this leads to consistent performance. The right mindset at the start of the game helps you be ready to play well at tip off. The right level of intensity, keen focus, and high confidence at the start of the game helps you get into the flow.

> "The mental side of the game is
> over 80% of the game.
> My mind is always going
> through situations and things that can
> happen on the floor to help us."
>
> — Lebron James

EXERCISE 1: ARE YOU MAKING THESE PREGAME MISTAKES?

Do you have the right mindset at the start of the game? For example, you've learned how to be proactive with your confidence before the game starts. Do you have proactive confidence or are you reacting to the warm-up or how well you are playing in the opening minutes of the game? Please place a checkmark next to each question you answer as "yes."

Are You Making These Pregame Mistakes?

Pregame Mental Mistakes	✓
1. Do you have strict expectations about your performance?	
2. Do you leave confidence to chance (you are not proactive)?	
3. Do you have self-doubt prior to the game?	
4. Do you focus on life's worries or hassles during games?	
5. Do you over-train or over-analyze before games?	
6. Do you take a practice mindset into games?	
7. Do you forget to think about a game plan or strategy?	
8. Do you psych yourself out by making comparisons to your competitors?	
9. Do you worry too much about what others think of you?	
10. Are you worried about statistics or performing poorly?	
11. Do you judge the quality of your warm-up performance?	
12. Do you worry too much about winning the game or not losing?	
13. Do you stress out if you can do you full or normal warm-up routine?	
14. Do you fail to be ready to perform with the A, B, or C-game, if needed?	
Please describe any other pregame mistakes:	

EXERCISE 2: WHAT'S YOUR PREGAME ROUTINE?

You already have a warmup routine, all athletes do. What specifically do you do before games to get ready and what's your team's warm up routine? **You might do the following:**

- Get dressed in game gear.
- Eat a pregame snack.
- Listen to favorite music.
- Do stretching exercises.
- Warm up physically with a few drills.
- Do team drills to warm up your dribble and shot.
- Team meeting with coach to discuss strategy.
- Think about how you might play against the person who's guarding you.

CHAPTER 8 – PREGAME PREPARATION

Please describe the steps in your pregame warm-up routine below. Include the steps you take (i.e., stretching, shooting, etc.) and anything you do mentally before the game (i.e., listen to music, rehearse your performance) from about one hour prior to the game:

1. ______________________________

2. ______________________________

3. ______________________________

4. ______________________________

5. ______________________________

6. ______________________________

7. ______________________________

One goal is to integrate mental skills into your team's warm-up routine. For example, you might prefer to listen to music before the game and visualize making plays on offense during the bus ride to the game or in the locker room.

SEVEN STEPS FOR PREGAME MENTAL PREPARATION

A pregame warm-up routine is not about having superstitions or rituals. Unlike pregame routines, superstitions are about what brings you luck. They don't apply sound science. Don't rely on lucky superstitions to bring you success. Rather, you want to use mental preparation strategies to help you feel confident and focused before each game.

Here are the top seven steps of your pregame routine you'll want to integrate into your warm-up routine:

Seven pregame mental preparation strategies:

1. Transition from life to sports and enter the role of the athlete.

2. Discard outcome expectations or strict demands for your game.

3. Be proactive with confidence prior to games.

4. Focus on execution or the process and not results.

5. Rehearse your performance and team plays.

6. Prepare your mind and body to trust in your skills.

7. Embrace the pregame jitters as helpful to your performance.

Many of these strategies will sound familiar to you as you've learned them in this program. Let's examine each of these mental strategies in more detail and how to integrate into your regular pregame warm-up...

STEP 1: TRANSITION FROM LIFE TO SPORTS

The pregame warm-up helps you get your game face on. This is a time to "park" potential distractions from school, friends, or family and focus on the game. You want to start each game without worries from your life into games, such as daily hassles, deadlines, and school assignments, etc. Commit fully to focusing on playing basketball for the next two hours.

EXERCISE 3: LIFE CHALLENGES YOU THINK ABOUT

What are your top three life challenges you bring onto the court, if any? Check all that apply to you. If one is not listed, please right it in the "other" space provided. You'll want to "park" stuff from your life outside basketball that you might bring into games.

Note: You can use this strategy for practice as well. How will you park these distractions from your life? You can't possibly change your life while you're on court during practice and games, so the best option is to set it aside for two hours. You can go back to solving these issues after the game.

Life Distractions

What Are Your Distractions	✓
School projects or assignments	
Relationship issues	
Friend argument	
Family life	
Work issues	
Money problems	
Other Issues:	

If you start to think about challenges, deadlines, or stuff in your life, use the Three R's to refocus (see workbook 2). Prior to warm-up, you want to "park" responsibilities from your life outside of basketball. You might write down what you have to accomplish after the game, leave it in your gym bag, and return to it after the game.

Your Pregame Tasks:

1. Write down any challenges or whatever is on your mind. For example, you might have assignments or stuff to do later that are on your mind.

2. Remind yourself to park any challenges until after the game.

3. Commit to entering the role of the athlete. Stay focused only on playing the game during the warm-up and game time.

STEP 2: MANAGE YOUR EXPECTATIONS

You've already learned about the dangers of having high expectations in sports in chapter 1. You want to perform free of pressure-packed expectations about your performance. Instead, your objective is to perform with (1) high self-confidence and (2) manageable objectives (or process goals).

"You want to perform free of pressure packed expectations about your performance."

Note any expectations you're feeling about the upcoming game. Commit to focusing on smaller objectives. Next, set two objectives to help you focus on the process, such as to focus on court awareness or drive hard to the basket when you have a lane.

What process goals will help you elevate your game? You can select from performance and mental game objectives:

1. **Performance goals:** making good passes, communicate with teammates, seeing the court well, etc.

2. **Mental game goals:** be decisive, stay in the present, or let go of mistakes quickly.

EXERCISE 4: YOUR EXPECTATIONS AND PROCESS GOALS

List two expectations you're feeling for this week's game:

1. ______________________________

2. ______________________________

What are two process goals you can focus on instead of your expectations?

1. ______________________________

2. ______________________________

Your Pregame Tasks:

1. Note any expectations you're feeling about your game or statistics.

2. Replace these expectations by focus on what's important to execute your position.

3. Focus on two simple process goals that will help you perform your position well.

STEP 3: BE PROACTIVE WITH CONFIDENCE

Confidence is how strongly you believe in the ability to execute your skills. You want to "fuel up" your confidence prior to the game. Remember, proactive confidence means you deserve to feel confident when you walk onto the court.

When you have self-doubt, question your preparation, or judge your performance during your warm-up, confidence can take a hit.

KEY POINT: The warm-up as just a warm-up—you don't have to win warm- ups. It's not a predictor of how you'll perform in the game.

Proactive confidence review:

1. Reviewing your confidence résumé

2. Reminding yourself of all the work you've done

3. Using positive self-talk proactively

4. Rehearsing your performance and your role

5. Thinking about the coach's game plan

EXERCISE 5: WHAT HELPS YOU FEEL CONFIDENT?

In Workbook 3, you listed several reasons why you deserve to feel confident. What can you add to your confidence resume this week, such as a good practice CHAPTER, that helps you feel confident?

1. ______________________________

2. ______________________________

You'll also want to reframe any pregame doubts you have. Do you have any doubts about your ability to perform well in the game?

Managing the confidence killers (chapter 4) is an important part of feeling confident too.

Your Pregame Tasks:

1. Review recent successful practices or games where you were confident.
2. Review your confidence resume and be confident in your performance.
3. Use positive self-talk statements to instill proactive confidence
4. Recognize and dispute any last-minute doubts you have prior to the game.

STEP 4: FOCUS IN THE MOMENT

Step 4 is to focus on one possession at a time. First, stay focused on your pregame warm-up for the game instead of the other team's talent. This is not the time to worry about outcomes, think about the other team's ability, or wonder who will be watching from the stands. Bring a process focus and high intensity to your pregame routine so you'll be ready when you start the game.

> "Bring a process focus and high intensity to your pregame routines so you'll be ready when you start the game."

EXERCISE 6: BE READY TO FOCUS IN THE GAME

What are two possible distractions for you in this week's game? Good mental preparation is about anticipating distractions and being ready to cope. Write two distractions below so you'll be ready to refocus if needed in the game.

1. ______________________________

2. ______________________________

Your Pregame Tasks:

1. Be aware of your common distractions that hurt focus.

2. How will you refocus when you think about these distractions?

3. When you recognize that you're distracted or thinking about results, refocus on your pregame warm-up.

4. What's your optimal physical intensity in the game? Get psyched up or stay calm depending on what you need to perform your best.

STEP 5: REHEARSE YOUR PERFORMANCE

The pregame warm-up is a great time to rehearse a few plays to instill confidence. You'll want to rehearse using a first-person perspective instead of from the perspective of seeing yourself on video (3rd person perspective). You might rehearse your game plan, being aggressive on the court, beating an opponent, or one mental skill, such as to let go of mistakes quickly.

KEY POINT: What you focus on, you improve in the game.

Here are a few examples of what you might rehearse before a game:

- Offensive: play decisively, be aggressive on drives, see the court well, or run team plays.

- Defensive: Quick feet on defense, guard your man aggressively, support teammates, go up for rebounds, or anticipate your opponent's move.

Retired professional basketball player Dre Baldwin would get ready by watching videos of favorite players having a great game and see himself playing the same way. He'd imagine how to play his opponents before the game. He would also listen to music to get up for the game, relax, or get angry.

EXERCISE 7: YOUR PREGAME REHEARSAL

Write two specific skills you can rehearse before the game. This might include driving hard to the basket, mental game skills, stopping your opponent on D, or common plays your team runs so you feel confident and ready to play.

1. ______________________________

2. ______________________________

Your Pregame Tasks:

1. Rehearse mental skills, such as coping with mistakes or performing with trust.

2. Use mental rehearsal to see and feel a successful game plan or strategy.

3. Rehearse yourself performing in real time, using a first-person perspective.

4. Experience yourself performing with confidence, composure and trust.

STEP 6: BE A PERFORMER AND TRUST YOUR SKILLS

Practice and preparation are over. Now it's time to have fun and compete! You don't want to practice your skills during the warm-up—transition into the game-time mindset. Trust the skills you bring to the game. Prepare to get the job done with the game you have that day!

Be ready to perform functionally, win ugly, or help your team with the skills you have today. Avoid judging your game or how you feel in the warm-up. Get the job done and find a way to help your team even with your B-game!

EXERCISE 8: TRUST IN YOUR SKILLS

Are you learning new moves in practice that make it harder to trust your skills in the game? Do you hesitate or become indecisive in games? Are you fearful of making mistakes and letting down teammates? All of these mindsets block your ability to perform athletically with trust.

What mindset will help you trust your skills today?

Do you need to let go of the practice mindset, play more athletically, react instead of overthink, be more decisive, or play functional ball?

1. ______________________________

2. ______________________________

3. ______________________________

The planning, preparation, and training is complete. You want to play by intuition or gut instincts during games. Now is the time to trust your basketball instincts you've developed— from years of practice and play. Keep it simple, believe in your ability, and be decisive in games to perform with trust.

Your Pregame Tasks:

1. Remind yourself that the warm-up is not a time to "practice."

2. Warm-up your shot, without judging how it feels or how many you make.

3. Remind yourself that you will focus better when the game begins.

4. Be ready to "win ugly" if you don't have your "A" game.

STEP 7: EMBRACE PREGAME JITTERS

Pregame jitters are a natural reaction for most athletes. Even the top NBA and WNBA players experience pregame jitters. Some players turn pregame jitters into stress or anxiety.

Instead, you want to think of pregame jitters as adrenaline or energy that will help you focus and boost your intensity. Pregame jitters also tell you that you care about your performance and want to do your best, which can help you embrace these feelings. *You want to welcome these feelings by accepting jitters as normal and helpful*.

Your Pregame Tasks:

1. Embrace the pregame jitters as a natural way to feel ready.

2. When you feel the jitters, instead of assuming you're anxious, focus on feeling pumped up and excited to perform well.
3. Tell yourself that you feel excited and amped up, not anxious.

4. Welcome the added adrenaline or energy and use it to your advantage to fuel your game.

SUMMARY

A pregame warm-up routine helps you mentally and physically prepare to perform well in every game. When you prepare consistently for each game, you'll improve your performance in games. Always remember that the warm-up is just a warm-up. You don't have to win warm-ups or perform your best during warm-ups! You don't need to hit every shot or feel perfect in the warm-up to perform well during the game.

If your warm-up is cut short for any reason, stay calm and do what you can with limited time. Rely on your motor memory (muscle memory) to perform your skills. You want to trust in your abilities at the start of the game, even if the warm-up does not feel right or go perfectly. Know that when you start the game, the pregame jitters and adrenaline can help you to focus better and thus perform well.

In the words of Pittsburgh Pirates hitting coach Gerald Perry, *"I tell the guys all the time if they're having a bad batting practice, 'I've never been approached by a reporter after a game asking me how my batting practice was.'"* Most athletes will focus better once they get into the game, and their performance will improve too.

PREGAME MENTAL PREP SUMMARY

Please remind yourself of the mental skills you are working on this week prior to practice and the game. Use the table below to help you mentally prepare for the game.

Mental Prep for Game

Mental Prep Area	Pregame Tasks
Enter Role of Athlete	☐ I acknowledge distractions from my life. ☐ I commit to "parking" life issues or hassles. ☐ I fully enter into & commit to role of athlete.
Game Plan or Strategy	☐ I study my opponent or opposing team's tendencies. ☐ I will use my strengths to win the game. ☐ I have set game plan to be successful in the game.
Proactive with Confidence	☐ I reviewed my list of reasons to be confident. ☐ I use positive self-talk statements to be confident. ☐ I shoot down any last-minute pregame doubts.
Set Process Goals	☐ I know what cues to focus on during performance. ☐ I set one or two process goals to focus on execution. ☐ I commit to focusing on one possession at a time.
Rehearse Performance	☐ I see and/or feel myself beating my opponent. ☐ I see and/or feel myself playing with confidence. ☐ I rehearse the first possession of the game.
Prepare to Trust	☐ I do not practice form during the warm-up. ☐ I do not judge the quality of my warm-up. ☐ Practice is complete for now – be a performer! Fun time!
Embrace the Butterflies	☐ I feel pumped and ready for games, not scared. ☐ I welcome butterflies as this is a sign that I am ready. ☐ I channel extra energy to help me focus at the start.

POST-GAME ASSESSMENT FOR CHAPTER 8

After your next scrimmage or game, please answer a few questions about your mental game. It's best if you answer them on the same day as your scrimmage or game.

1. What are two things you did well today with your mental game and performance?

2. What are two things you would like to improve for the next game?

3. How well did you use your pregame routine to mentally prepare by letting go of expectations, focusing on the process, and trusting your skills?

4. What assumptions did you make about the quality of your warm-up prior to the game, if any?

5. How well did you focus on one play at a time and not think ahead in today's game?

6. How often did you trust in your skills today and focus on getting the job done?

7. Based on your answers here, what mental game skills do you want to improve for the next game?

MY NOTES

MY NOTES

MY NOTES

MY NOTES

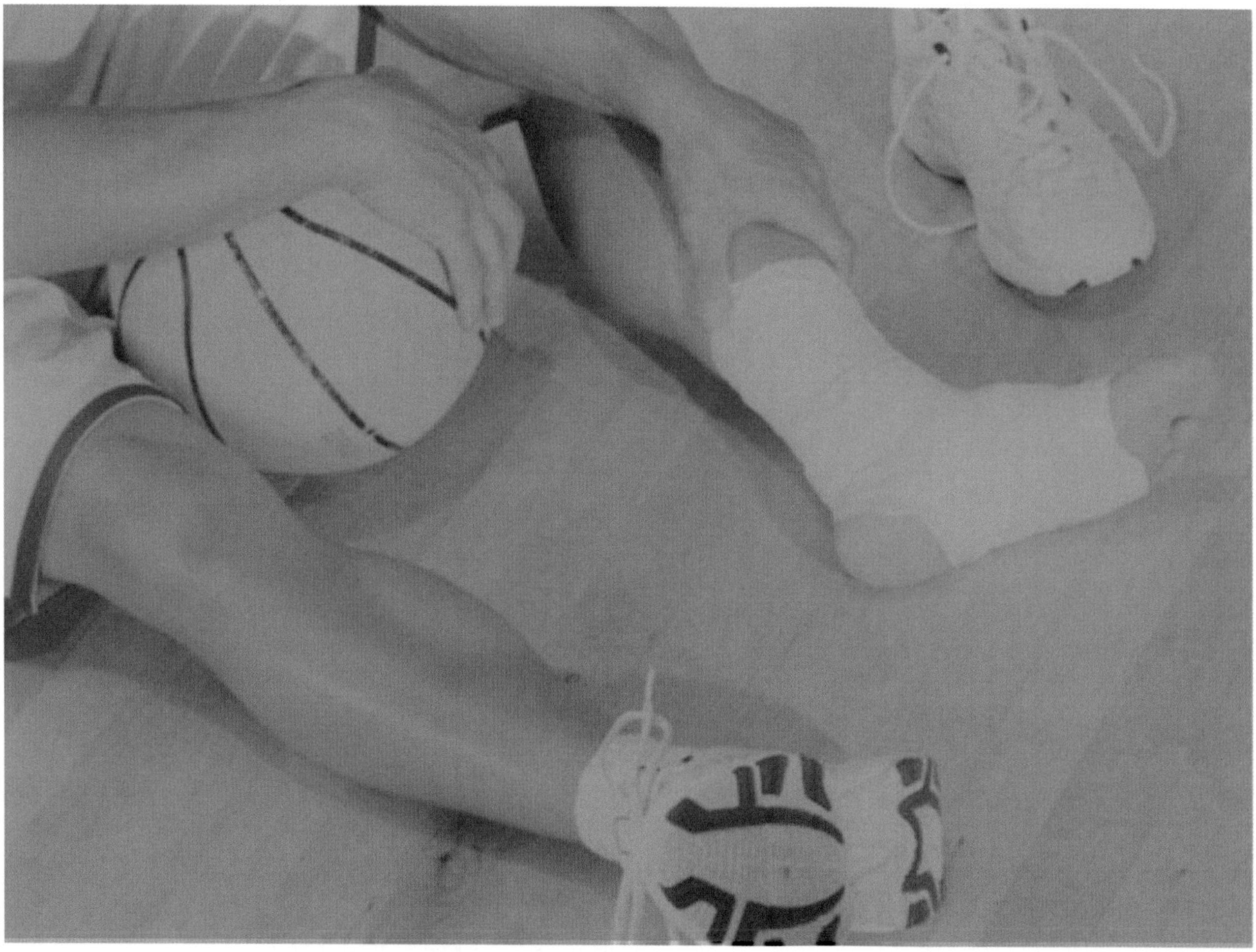

CHAPTER 9

RETURN AFTER INJURY

MENTALLY PREPARING ATHLETES TO RETURN TO PLAY FOLLOWING INJURY

CHAPTER Objective

In this chapter, you'll learn how to be mentally prepared to return to sport after full recovery from injury—with confidence and trust in your game.

What You Need to Know

After you're medically cleared to practice and compete, you're probably eager to return to sport. Although you may be 100% physically ready to return, you might not be mentally ready to return. You want to be sure that you are both mentally and physically ready to return to perform or play.

Many challenges come with recovery and return to sport, both physical and mental. You'll learn about the most common mental game challenges that athletes encounter. These range from frustration and anger, doubt about your skills after you return, or even fears that you may not return to the same performance level. You'll also learn four mental game skills to help you return to play successfully.

"You want to be sure that you are both mentally and physically ready to return to play."

Challenges Returning to Sport After Full Recovery

What are your top concerns about returning to practice and competition? Please rate yourself based on your situation. Understanding how you might react when you return can help you be mentally prepared. Below are the top 10 challenges for athletes returning to play post-recovery.

Continue to the exercise on the following page...

Exercise 1: What Are Your Challenges Returning to Sport?

Please grade your challenges or concerns in the table below from 1 to 5 (1-strongly disagree, 2-disagree, 3-moderate, 4-agree, 5-strongly agree).

Challenge	Grade
Fear of re-injury. Increased anxiety while playing, focusing unnecessarily on your recovered body part, or heavily taping the recovered area.	1 2 3 4 5
Playing cautiously or safely. Holding back because you are unsure about your skills or how well your body will hold up.	1 2 3 4 5
Avoiding plays or skills similar to the one that you got hurt on. During practice or in the weight room, you avoid executing the skill that got you hurt in the first place.	1 2 3 4 5
Not trusting in your skills or your recovered body part. Not attempting to do skills you are capable of doing 100%.	1 2 3 4 5
Feeling isolated from the team. Feeling as though you are no longer part of the team or the team's mission.	1 2 3 4 5
Not meeting your expectations for performance when you return. Worries about not performing up to your preinjury level.	1 2 3 4 5
Not meeting others' expectations for your performance or return. Are you worried about losing your team or being benched because you aren't playing up to how others think you should be playing?	1 2 3 4 5
Worries of letting down your team, coach or parents. Feeling like you aren't going to perform well enough from others or that you are no longer good enough to hold your position.	1 2 3 4 5
Worry about losing your reputation as the player you once were. Not having respect from others or losing your position within the team.	1 2 3 4 5
Not adapting well to the increased intensity of competition. Struggling with the physical strain, fatigue, and challenges when returning to sport.	1 2 3 4 5
Other Challenges/Concerns/Issues:	1 2 3 4 5

MANAGE EXPECTATIONS

When you return to your sport, you want to be ready to take on these challenges head-on to perform with confidence and composure. The objective is to perform athletically by trusting your skills and body.

Many athletes describe playing athletically or freely as "flow" as if their performance feels effortless. If you have high expectations for your performance, worry about re-injury, or get caught up in your new role on the team, it's harder to perform with trust and find a flow.

"High expectations are your unwritten standards for success or failure."

Step 1: Manage Your Expectations

Do you have any hidden expectations about your level of play or what your teammates expect when you return? When you return to sports after rehab, you might expect to perform as well as before the injury. However, you don't want to place high expectations on your performance.

High expectations are your unwritten standards for success or failure, which can hurt your confidence if you fail to reach them. High expectations, those you maintain yourself and those you perceive from others, can also cause you to feel pressure. When athletes perceive pressures from others (coaches, teammates, or making a team), they return to play before they are mentally or physically ready.

A Mental Game Formula for Success

The objective is to perform without the demands and judgments caused by your high expectations for performance. Instead, your objective is to perform with (1) high self- confidence and (2) focus on manageable objectives, or what we call process goals.

Three Steps in The Formula For Success:

1. Uncover and flush out strict expectations or demands that affect your self-confidence negatively and create undue pressure.
2. Harness the power of confidence and learn how to have high confidence that's void of expectation.
3. Replace high expectations with process goals or small objectives. You aim to immerse yourself in process goals while avoiding turning them into expectations.

1. What Are Your Expectations About Returning?

Below are some common expectations that athletes maintain. Place a check next to all that apply to you. If one of your expectations is not listed, please list it in the "other" space provided.

Expectations	✓
1. I should perform at the same level as before the injury.	
2. I should be able to play through any pain.	
3. I should perform with the same level of confidence I had before.	
4. I should beat this opponent because I've beaten them before.	
5. I should sacrifice my physical/mental health to make this team.	
6. I should not be nervous before the game.	
7. I need to catch up to my teammates because of the time missed	
8. Others think I should be playing up to my previous level.	
Others:	

2. Replace with Process Goals

Your goal should be to perform without any expectations, good or bad. The objective is to replace your expectations with more manageable tasks or process goals. Using the expectations listed in the exercise above, replace each expectation with more manageable process goals. Process goals provide a roadmap for improvement and help players stay focused on the controllable aspects of their performance.

Process goals: Specific, measurable, and controllable actions or behaviors that players can focus on to improve their overall performance. Unlike outcome goals, which are centered on the result of a game, process goals emphasize techniques and procedures that lead to success.

Qualities of a good process goal.

1. Simple (technique or procedure).
2. Help you focus on your role or what you can control.
3. Focus on what you want to accomplish instead of what you want to avoid.

Here are examples of process goals for basketball players:

- Fight over ball screens with 100% effort.
- Communicate on defense/ Call out screens and cutters.
- Look for open lanes.
- Keep feet moving on defense.
- Have my hands ready to shoot.
- Keep my elbow in and follow through on the shot.
- Trust in my abilities.
- Be in the moment.
- Be aggressive on the drive.
- Find a body to box out.
- Look at the rim before passing.
- Ball fake.
- Relax and have fun
- Fully commit to shooting when open.
- Follow your shot into the net; look for rebound

- **Mental Game Goals:** Stay in the present, move on after any mistakes, and trust in your skills, visualize for 3 minutes before the game, take deep breaths when feeling overwhelmed, and review my "why" before the game.

Step 2: Focus on the Process

Improving your concentration is a top priority for any athlete, especially after recovery. Having good concentration means that you're able to focus on the process and the correct cues that will help you perform.

After returning, you may focus more on irrelevant things. You might have distracting thoughts of letting down your team, fear of being benched or losing your spot on the team, fear of pain or re-injury, worrying about others' expectations, or not meeting your previous level of play.

"Your goal should be to perform without any expectations, good or bad."

When you focus on the process, you concentrate on the present moment (the here and now). Performing your best in any sport occurs when you focus on the execution of a skill instead of worrying about results or outcomes. For example, instead of thinking about the pain, you may feel from sliding into home, you want to focus on your slide and getting to home plate.

Three steps for focusing on the process:

1. Define what you want to focus on (performance cues).
2. Be aware of your common distractions.
3. Stay immersed in the process.

Performance cues are thoughts, images, or feelings that help you plan and execute a skill. Step one will ask you to think about the performance cues in your sport, which you'll learn to do here. These might include planning or preparing for a skill, things that help you execute your roles, such as attacking the ball or field awareness.

What are your performance cues?

1. ______________________________

2. ______________________________

3. ______________________________

4. ______________________________

Likewise, you'll also want to know what's not important to think about when performing, or, your distractions. A distraction can be any thought, image, or feeling that takes your focus away from what's important – executing a skill or play. For example, thinking about whether or not making a specific move will stress your body is not relevant because it distracts your mind from thinking about execution.

What are your common distractions:

1. ______________________________

2. ______________________________

3. ______________________________

4. ______________________________

When your mind wanders to distractions, you want to refocus. To do this, you'll use a simple strategy called "The Three-R's for Refocusing," which includes:

1. **Recognize** — that you are distracted or not focused in the moment.
2. **Regroup** — tell yourself to stop and get back to the task.
3. **Refocus** — on the task-relevant performance cues of the current shot.

The Three R's for refocusing helps you regain your focus quickly after a distraction. When you notice you are distracted or off-task, you must act on this and not allow your mind to wander for an inning, period, game, or match!

Step 3: Proactive Confidence

Self-confidence is how strongly you believe in your ability to execute any skill or task. High confidence helps to improve your overall mental game. Confidence enables you to let go of mistakes quicker and stay calm and composed. It also allows you to take risks and play boldly instead of tentatively.

You develop confidence over many years of practice and performance. It comes from past performances, success, training, preparation, and mental toughness. You can also derive confidence from the belief that you have strong physical skills that will help you be successful. After rehab, believing in your abilities to execute your skills can be more difficult.

"When your mind wanders to distractions, you want to refocus."

Your confidence might not be high when returning to play because you have:

- Fear of re-injury or focusing too much on your healed body.
- Worries about your body not being strong enough.
- Doubt about how well you will perform or worry about not performing up to your previous level.
- Changes in mechanics and muscle memory.
- Pressure to return by the start of a season.

Your confidence might not be high when returning to play because you have (continued):

- Comparing yourself to other athletes' when you return.
- Comparing yourself to your previous level of performance.

Two parts to high confidence:

1. Be proactive with confidence instead of reactive. ProacWve confidence means taking responsibility for your confidence level.
2. Be mindful of the confidence killers and how to overcome them.

Proactive Confidence

The first way to be proactive with your confidence is to understand your athletic strengths and abilities and focus on those. Your task is to write a confidence résumé, which includes your past accomplishments, successes during or post rehab, experiences, strengths, and anything else that supports your confidence.

Use the questions below to help you get started with your confidence résumé:

1. What are your strengths as an athlete in your sport?
2. What have others complimented you about (e.g., your technique, commitment, determination, ability to overcome adversity, etc.)?
3. What have you accomplished in your sport that you are proud of (e.g., local, state, and national competition, etc.)?
4. How would you describe your game to others if you took the most positive stance?
5. What can you say about your practice routine that gives you confidence?
6. What can you say about your commitment or work ethic in sports?
7. What can you say about the coaching that helps you feel confident?
8. What can you say about your mental game that gives you confidence in your ability?
9. What can you say about your fitness, diet, or other routines that provide you confidence?

My Confidence Résumé

Use the space below to write your confidence résumé:

1. ______________________________

2. ______________________________

3. ______________________________

4. ______________________________

5. ______________________________

6. ______________________________

7. ______________________________

8. ______________________________

9. ______________________________

10. ______________________________

11. ______________________________

12. ______________________________

Manage the Confidence Killers

You also want to be aware of what hurts your confidence. Below is a pre-test to help you identify what might kill your confidence. Please check all that apply to you in the following table.

Can You Relate to These?	✓
1. You maintain strict expectations about your performance.	
2. You question your ability to perform (self-doubt).	
3. You struggle to prepare or lack a game plan competing.	
4. You compare yourself to other athletes.	
5. You worry about what others think of you.	
6. You need to be perfect or play all the time perfectly.	
7. You feel like you always choke or underperform in competition.	
8. You dwell on mistakes or mishaps during competitions.	
9. You get anxious or frustrated after a bad warm-up.	
10. You focus only on the negatives after not performing well.	
11. You always talk negatively about yourself or your performance.	
12. You call yourself names after a poor performance.	
13. You feel like you can't perform under pressure.	
14. You think performing well is luck or that your competition just wasn't good.	

Based on your answers to the above test, you'll want to work with your mental coach to overcome these confidence killers when returning to sports.

Step 4: Trust Your Skills

Trust is letting go of consciously controlling your performance and instead relying on motor memory (or what coaches call muscle memory). When you return to competition, trust in your skills helps you perform your best.

Your performance is cautious or safe when you don't perform with trust. If you fear pain or weakness in your body, you might hold back and perform tentatively. You might feel less confident in the recovered body part. You might even be unsure that you are 100% physically ready to return. Any fear or lack of confidence can hurt your trust.

Did you change mechanics during rehab or recovery? When you change or re-learn mechanics; you can lose trust in your skills in the short term.

How Do You Lose Trust?

Your next step is understanding what causes you to lose trust in your skills as you return to play. Below are eight common scenarios that can cause your trust to break down. Please check all statements that apply to your situation:

Trust Breakdowns	✓
1. Being too mechanical — thinking too much about your technique or form.	
2. **Over aiming** — steering or guiding a shot to the target; trying too hard to be precise.	
3. **Overcontrolling your skills** — trying too hard to protect your body from injury.	
4. **Exertng more effort than optimal** — trying too hard to go big.	
5. **Being tentative with your game** — trying to avoid pain or re-injury; playing it safe.	
6. **Fear of Reinjury** — worry, fear, or apprehension about the recovered body part.	
7. **Perfectionism**— trying too hard to perfect your performance.	
8. **Over-analysis** — trying to understand why you made an error and fixing it.	
9. **Lack of confidence** — when you don't have full confidence in your body to hold up.	
10. **Indecision** — wishy-washy and get stuck between deciding on what play to make.	

Improving Trust in Your Skills

Here are the top three mental game strategies you'll want to master to improve trust in games:

1. Be decisive when performing.
2. Simplify your thinking: Less is better.
3. Use the skills you have that day.

Let's examine each of these strategies...

"Being decisive in competition—instead of hesitant—can improve trust in your skills."

Be Decisive With Your Game

Being decisive in competition—instead of hesitant—can improve trust in your skills. Being decisive means going with your instincts when performing instead of second-guessing what you are doing. This means you go with your first plan and make quick, intuitive decisions.

When you return to play, what might cause you to be indecisive or second-guess? **Some examples are:**

- Fear of your body not holding up.
- Fear of re-injury (especially during similar play).
- Uncertainty of whether or not you can make a play, shot, or routine.
- Indecision about coming to a shot, play, or pass.
- Worry about not being as good as you once were.
- Fear of injuring another body part.
- Worry about being benched or losing your position on the team.
- Trying too hard to make the perfect play, or overthinking your game.
- Fear of embarrassment and what others may think of you.

Simplify Your Thinking: Less is Better

Simplifying your performance means quieting the mind and not overthinking your skills. An overactive mind may sound like this: *"Oh my gosh, I am up next, I hope I don't get hurt again, I don't want to go, my shoe is untied, everyone is watching me, can I make this play, will my coach bench me if I don't?"*

A quiet mind sounds more like this: *"Breathe in, breathe out, focus only on the process..."*

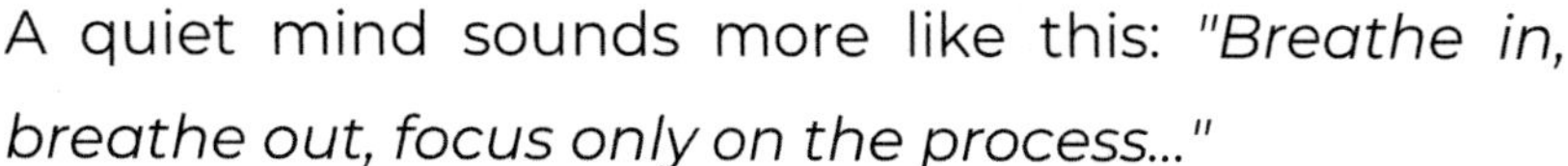

Use the Skills You Have Today

SWck to your "bread and butter" play, shot, or skill. This is the skill that's working that day. Use what's working rather than needing to perform the "correct" or perfect way. Know that you have done all you can to prepare and do what it takes to get the job done in competition today.

Shift your focus to functional performance rather than perfection. Acknowledge that, as a human, mistakes are inevitable, and understand that it takes time for your body to play at its full potential.

A professional tennis coach, Brad Gilbert, refers to a functional mindset as "winning ugly." Winning ugly is using whatever skills you can that day to get the job done.

Summary

Once you are medically cleared to return to play, you want to be mentally ready. When returning to sports, you might have many mental game challenges. When you return, you may doubt your skill level or even fear that you might not return to your prior performance level.

You learned four important mental game skills to help you return to sport successfully. First, you must **set your expectations aside** and focus on improving your game one practice at a time. Second, you want to **focus on the process** and what's important for your role on the team. Third, you want to **be proactive with your confidence** and manage any lingering confidence killers. Lastly, you want to learn to **trust your skills**, especially if you made any technical changes to your game. Be patient with your return, as "Rome was not built overnight."

THIS WEEKS ACTION PLANS

Please apply the mental strategies you learned this week to practice and competition using the action plans below.

1. **Awareness Exercise**

   Note any doubt, indecision, or expectations before your practice. Keep your expectations and doubts in check using positive self-talk. Avoid comparing your performance now with your pre-injury level. Set small objectives each day that you can easily meet.

2. **Practice Plan**

   As you get more practice time after your return, work on your trusting skills, especially if you have made any recent technical changes. As your fitness and strength improve, begin to trust in your skills 100% during scrimmages and drills.

3. **Game-Time Application**

   Stay in the moment when competing. Avoid thinking about "what ifs," such as, *"What if I push hard...will my body hold up?"* It will help if you put your fear aside before competition so you can play intuitively and athletically. Use the skills you have today, no matter how imperfect you feel, and let go of the need to perform perfectly.

MENTAL GAME ASSESSMENT CHAPTER 9

After your practice or competition this week, please answer a few questions about your mental game. It's best if you answer them on the same day as your scrimmage or game.

1. What were two things you did well this week with your mental approach to practice or competition?

2. What are two things you would like to improve for the next week's practice?

3. How well did you let go of any expectations about your performance this week?

4. How well did you focus on the process and not get ahead of yourself? What distracted you related to how your body felt if anything?

5. How confident did you feel this week in practice and or competition? What doubts did you have, if any?

6. How would you rate your ability to trust in your skills (0 to 100%)? What moves or skills were hard to trust?

7. Based on your answers to the questions above, how can you improve your mental game for next week?

MY NOTES

MY NOTES

MY NOTES

MY NOTES

CHAPTER 10

GOAL SETTING

DEVELOPING YOUR ROADMAP FOR SUCCESS.

CHAPTER OBJECTIVE

Learn the best practices for effectively setting goals and break them down into actions, behaviors, and habits that pave the way for successfully achieving your goals.

WHAT YOU NEED TO KNOW

Goal setting is the #1 mental skill used by athletes and proven to aide in performance improvement. A **goal** is defined ***as an objective or aim of action, and aspired task or accomplishment.*** Essentially, its a target set to achieve a desired result in the future. As an athlete, setting goals is one of the most important steps to improving your performance and achieving an aspired objective.

Goal setting is like crafting a roadmap. It involves creating a plan and then actively taking steps to make your desired outcome a reality. Goal setting is a common practice many people use in many aspects of their lives including sports, school, work, etc.

Several advantages come with setting goals like giving you a clear path, a sense of direction, focus, motivation, increased resilience, a way to track progress, and a form of accountability.

Many athletes, including Olympic gold medalist, use goal-setting tools to enhance their performance and stay motivated throughout the season. However, many athletes are unaware of the best practices that lead to success. This workbook will introduce you to effective goal-setting practices.

> I'm a firm believer in goal setting. Step by step. I can't see any other way of accomplishing anything.
>
> — Michel Jordan

WHEN TO SET GOALS

Goal setting is a powerful tool that you can use at different points in your basketball journey. It's most effective when done before the season kicks off in **pre-season training,** during the **off-season for post-season workouts**, and sometimes in the **middle of the season**. In the middle of the season, you might need to tweak your goals to make sure you're on track for your long-term objectives. Coaches, trainers, and parents can provide useful feedback during this process. Remember, goal setting isn't just about getting better at basketball; it's also a smart approach for recovering from injuries. Setting **rehabilitation goals** helps you stay motivated and make progress towards returning to the player you were before the injury.

TEST YOUR GOAL SETTING SKILLS

Before we dive into sharpening your goal-setting skills, let's put them to the test. After you finish the assessment, add up the numbers you circled for each question to calculate your score. Then, check where you stand in the rankings.

Score	Results
53-65	You have excellent goal-setting skills and practices. Our workbook can help you further refine and expand upon these skills.
40-52	You've already built a solid foundation of goal-setting skills. Applying more structure and best practices from this workbook can significantly enhance your effectiveness in goal setting.
27-39	It seems like you have some experience with goal setting, but there's room to enhance its effectiveness. This workbook is an excellent guide to fortify your foundation and advance your goal-setting skills.
10-26	Goal setting may not be your forte, but you're in the right place. This workbook will walk you through honing this skill and teach you the best practices to become an excellent goal setter.

EXERCISE 1: TEST YOUR GOAL SETTING SKILLS

Please rate yourself on best goal-setting practices using the table below from 1 to 5 (1-strongly disagree, 2- disagree, 3-moderate, 4-agree, 5-strongly agree).

Goal Setting Statement	Rate Yourself
My goals are detailed and specific	1 2 3 4 5
I break down my goals in small steps.	1 2 3 4 5
I write down my goals.	1 2 3 4 5
I imagine (visualize) myself accomplishing my goals.	1 2 3 4 5
I spend time working towards my goals on the weekly basis.	1 2 3 4 5
I track my progress as I work towards accomplishing my goal.	1 2 3 4 5
My goals are important and meaningful to me.	1 2 3 4 5
My goals challenge me to be my best or learn a new skill.	1 2 3 4 5
I set deadlines for me to accomplish my goals.	1 2 3 4 5
I celebrate milestones as I work toward accomplishing my goals.	1 2 3 4 5
I prepare for potential obstacles I may encounter.	1 2 3 4 5
I seek support in helping me accomplish my goal. (Example: accountability partner or teammate that comes to the gym with me.)	1 2 3 4 5
I research what it takes to achieve a goal before I set it.	1 2 3 4 5

TYPES OF GOALS

Most athletes are familiar with long-term and short-term goals. But as an athlete, it's more effective to concentrate on these three types of goals: **outcome, performance, and process goals.** According to sports psychology research, there's a connected path among process, performance, and outcome goals. Successfully achieving your process goals improves your chances of reaching performance goals. Similarly, accomplishing performance goals enhances the likelihood of attaining your outcome goal. In essence, it's about taking step-by-step actions to enhance your overall performance.

Break your goals into small steps you can take every day, so they won't overwhelm you. Think big, but start small.

— David Young

Outcome Goal: Goals focus on final results. This goal is typically a long-term goal that is vague and where an athlete wants to get to.
Example 1: My goal is to win a tournament/championship
Example 2: Improve shooting to help my team win conference championship.

Performance Goal: A goal that focuses on improving the quality of performance. It's where the athlete sets a standard of performance and determines the criteria to improve.
Example 1: Shoot 80% from the free-throw line in games and practice.
Example 2: Attempt 10 shots per game and average 50%.

Process Goal: Specific, measurable, and controllable actions or behaviors that players can focus on to improve their overall performance. Unlike outcome goals, which are centered on the result of a game, process goals emphasize techniques and procedures that lead to success.
Example1 : My goal is to keep my elbow in and have a high arc when I shoot.
Example2 : Shoot 100 jump shots after practice or spend X amount of hours shooting per week.

GOAL SETTING EXAMPLES

Process goals are the building blocks for creating new habits and developing skills that lead to improved performance. They provide a foundation for improvement and help players stay focused on the controllable aspects of their performance. These guidelines help you write out effective process goals and provide you with examples.

Process goals: Specific, measurable, and controllable actions or behaviors that players can focus on to improve their overall performance. Unlike outcome goals, which are centered on the result of a game, process goals emphasize techniques and procedures that lead to success.

Qualities of a good process goal.

1. Simple (technique, skill, or procedure).
2. Help you focus on skill development and improvements you can control.
3. Focus on what you want to accomplish instead of what you want to avoid.

Here are examples of process goals for basketball players:

- Fight over ball screens with 100% effort.
- Communicate on defense/ Call out screens and cutters.
- Look for open lanes.
- Keep feet moving on defense.
- Have my hands ready to shoot.
- Keep my elbow in and follow through on the shot.
- See man and ball when in help.
- Be in the moment.
- Stay low when dribbling.
- Find a body to box out.
- Look at the rim before passing.
- Ball fake.
- Shoot X amount of shots after practice.
- Fully commit to shooting when open.
- Follow your shot into the net; look for rebound

• **Mental Game Goals:** Stay in the present, move on after any mistakes, and trust in your skills, visualize for 3 minutes before the game, take deep breaths when feeling overwhelmed, and review my "why" before the game.

EXERCISE 2: GOAL SETTING

Instructions: Create an outcome goal and break it down into performance, and process goals using the boxes below.

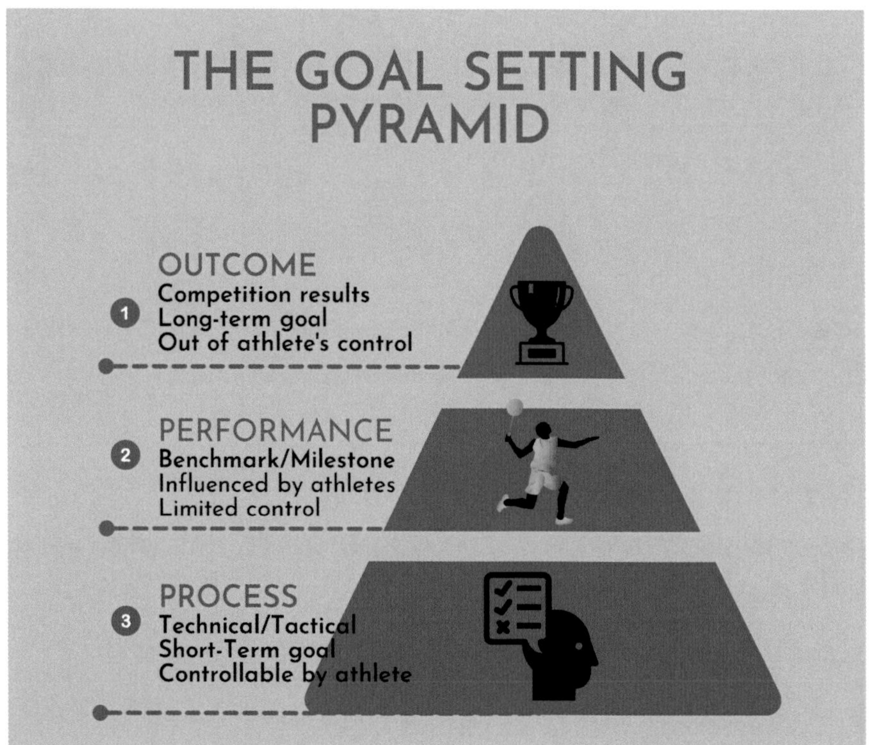

Outcome Goal (Result/ Final state)	
Performance Goal (Improvement goal)	
Process Goal (Technique/preparation)	

EXERCISE 3: GOAL SETTING

Create an outcome goal and break it down into performance, and process goals.

OUTCOME GOAL:

EXAMPLE: Improve free-throw shooting or strengthen on ball defense.

____

PERFORMANCE GOAL:

EXAMPLE: Shoot 80% from free-throw in practice half of my game., average 6 free-throw attempts each game, and make 50 free-throws at the end of each practice.

1. ____
2. ____
3. ____

PROCESS GOALS:

EXAMPLE: Hold follow through when shooting, increase arc on shot, spend 1 hour a week shooting free-throws.

1. ____
2. ____
3. ____

Goal Setting Tip: This format for goal setting can apply to more than your basketball performance. It can also apply to your mental game too. Workbook 8: Page 5 has a list of process goals as a template to assist you. Other mental game goals include staying in the present, moving on after any mistakes, trusting in your skills, visualizing for 3 minutes before the game, taking deep breaths when feeling overwhelmed, and reviewing my "why" before the game.

S.M.A.R.T GOALS

Another format used to write goals is through acronym S.M.A.R.T. SMART goals are Specific, Measurable, Action-oriented, Realistic, and Time-bound. This acronym offers clear guidelines for developing goals that are more achievable and effective.

Specific: Your goal should be clear and intentional, answering the questions: What, Why, and How? This helps in focusing efforts and clearly defines what needs to be achieved.

Measurable: Include how you will measure progress and how you will know you achieved your goal.

Action-Oriented: Determine task-specific steps, habits, or systems to accomplish this goal.

Realistic: Make sure your goal challenges you but still attainable. Consider these questions: Is this goal achievable for me? Do I have the resources and support to accomplish this goal?

Time-Bound: Establish a deadline and timeline to accomplish the goal.

Example:

- **Goal:** At the end of 90 days I want to improve my made free throw percentage from 70% to 80% by shooting with a higher arch and holding the follow-through.
    - **Specific:** Improve made free throw percentage.
    - **Measurable:** Increase by 10% from 70% to 80%.
    - **Action-Oriented:** Shooting with a higher arch and holding the follow-through.
    - **Realistic:** Yes, increasing free throw percentage by 10% over 90 days is realistic.
    - **Time-bound:** At the end of 90 days.

EXERCISE 4: SMART GOALS

Step 1: SMART goals worksheet #1

Consider the question on SMART goals worksheet #1. Then write out your goal in the space below.

GOAL: ____

____

____

Step 2: Is my goal SMART?

Review the criteria for SMART goals listed on page 8 and use the checklist to identify if your goal meets the criteria to be considered SMART.

____SPECIFIC ____ MEASURABLE ____ ACTION-ORIENTED

____REALISTIC ____TIMEBOUND

Step 3: Edit your goal

Use SMART goals worksheet #2 to write out and updated version of your goal. Putting each element of the goal in its designated box like the example listed below.

- **Goal:** At the end of 90 days I want to improve my made free throw percentage from 70% to 80% by shooting with a higher arch and holding the follow-through.
  - **Specific:** Improve made free throw percentage.
  - **Measurable:** Increase by 10% from 70% to 80%.
  - **Action-Oriented:** Shooting with a higher arch and holding the follow-through.
  - **Realistic:** Yes, increasing free throw percentage by 10% over 90 days is realistic.
  - **Time-bound:** At the end of 90 days.

SMART GOALS WORKSHEET # 1

Worksheet #1 :Instructions: Consider the following questions when writing out your goals. Use the next page to write out your SMART goal.

S	**SPECIFIC**	A. What exactly do you want to achieve? B. Why is this important to me? C. How will I accomplish this goal?
M	**MEASURABLE**	A. How will you track progress? B. What are important signs things are going well or not? C. How will you know when the goal is accomplished?
A	**ACTION-ORIENTED**	A. What task or behaviors do I need to take towards accomplishing this goal? B. What new habits do I need to establish to help me accomplish this goal?
R	**REALISTIC**	A. Is the goal achievable? B. What factors may prevent you from accomplishing your goal? C. Do I have the resources and support to accomplish this goal?
T	**TIME-BOUND**	A. When will you start working on the goal? B. What is the date/time-frame you wan to accomplish this goal? C. Are there any milestones or checkpoints along the way?

SMART GOALS WORKSHEET #2

GOAL: ____

S	
M	
A	
R	
T	

GOAL SETTING BEST PRACTICES

In this chapter, we'll explore different frameworks for goal setting. However, before delving into those frameworks, it's crucial to understand and apply best practices for goal setting. Here's a list of dos and don'ts for effective goal setting."

GOAL SETTING DO'S AND DON'TS

Write it down

Writing down your goal enhances your ability to remember it and provides a clear reference point for tracking and reassessing your progress. Studies have shown that individuals who document their goals are 33%-42% more likely to achieve them.

Use Positive working

Make sure the words you use when writing your goal are positive. Describe actions or behaviors you want to achieve, not things you want to avoid. For example, "See open hands and name across the jersey before passing into post" is a positive way to frame your goal, instead of saying "No turnovers when making a pass entry to the post."

Review and assess your progress

Review and assess your progress toward the goal regularly. It's a good practice to reassess your goal to ensure it remains realistic, achievable, and challenging enough to facilitate your improvements. Additionally, when your assessing your progress make sure you celebrate the small wins. Taking time to acknowledge and celebrate incremental progress fuels motivation, focus, perseverance, and resilience

Get support

Being in a supportive environment boosts motivation and encouragement to maintain commitment, discipline, and consistency. It also makes you, as a player, accountable for accomplishing your goals. For example, share your goal with a friend, teammate, or coach, and have them assist you or remind you about the goal.

Start Small

Break your goals down into small, attainable steps. Use process goals that lead to increased performance and desired outcomes. This helps you stay motivated, focused, and consistent.

Set S.M.A.R.T Goals

Make sure your goals are SMART: **S**pecific, **M**easurable, **A**ction-oriented, **R**ealistic, and **T**imebound. See page 8 for more information on SMART goals.

GOAL SETTING BEST PRACTICES

In this chapter, we'll explore different frameworks for goal setting. However, before delving into those frameworks, it's crucial to understand and apply best practices for goal setting. Here's a list of dos and don'ts for effective goal setting."

GOAL SETTING DO'S AND DON'TS

DON'TS

Visualize Sucess

Spend time (2-5 min) imagining yourself achieving your goals. Visualization can boost confidence, motivation, and performance.

Prepare for Obstacles

Identify potential obstacles and make a plan to prepare for them. For example, what if you don't have access to a shooting facility? What if you don't have a shooting partner? What if you're required to skip a workout, etc? Develop a plan of action for how you will approach potential obstacles, catering to your goals.

Make it Routine

RMake it routine: Incorporate the goal-related action or habit into your daily routine. This helps in forming habits, maintaining consistency, and discipline, ultimately leading to success. Also, prominently display your goals in a visible location to serve as a daily reminder.

Too Easy

Setting goals that don't challenge you to grow as an athlete provides no real benefit and may result in a lack of motivation or commitment to the goal.

Too Many

BSetting too many goals at once can overwhelm you and limit your focus, often leading to individuals abandoning or stopping the pursuit of the goal. It's better to prioritize a few key goals.

Do it Alone

Often, athletes try to achieve their goals in isolation. Research shows that those who share their goals with others and enlist an accountability partner are more likely to successfully accomplish them. Additionally, they are more motivated and feel supported when facing challenges. So, remember, don't try to go it alone.

GOAL SETTING BEST PRACTICES

In this chapter, we'll explore different frameworks for goal setting. However, before delving into those frameworks, it's crucial to understand and apply best practices for goal setting. Here's a list of dos and don'ts for effective goal setting."

GOAL SETTING DO'S AND DON'TS

Expecting Perfection

Expecting perfection can lead to frustration, hesitancy, fear or failure, loss of motivation, and have an overall negative impact on your mental health. Embrace the learning opportunities from mistakes viewing them as a natural part of the journey towards success and accomplishing your goal.

Setting Goals Based in Fear

Avoid setting goals out of fear or a desire to avoid negative consequences. Goals should be driven by positive wording and working towards and accomplishment.

Avoiding Timelines

A goal without a deadline is just a dream" - Robert Herjavec. Goals lacking deadlines diminish motivation, accountability, and commitment. When setting a goal, it's crucial to make it timebound (the T in SMART goals).

Ignore the Importance of Planning

Setting goals is just the beginning. It's challenging to make progress without a well-thought-out plan of action, or step-by-step plan. And often times results in a lack of commitment and motivation to accomplish the goal.

Out of Sight out of Mind

Athletes who don't regularly revisit their goals often forget about them. Additionally, they miss the chance to effectively track progress and celebrate small wins, leading to decreased motivation, commitment, discipline, and accountability.

Losing Sight of Your Why

During times of frustration, fatigue, and challenges athletes lose sight of their why. It's important to remember the intention of why you set the goal in the first place. Understanding the underlying motivation can keep you focused and motivated.

EXERCISE 5: BAD PRACTICES

Reflecting on the goal-setting do's and don'ts list from earlier pages, identify the top three "don'ts" or bad practices you've used in the past that hindered your goal achievement. Then outline how you plan to avoid these pitfalls in the future.

Bad Practice	Plan of action
Example: Doing it alone	**Example: I will tell my coach and have my teammate (insert name) as an accountability partner.**

EXERCISE 6: BEST PRACTICES

List 3 of the goal setting best practices you plan to implement in your routine.

✓ ______________________________

✓ ______________________________

✓ ______________________________

EXERCISE 7: VISUALIZE YOUR GOAL

Visualization or mental imagery is the practice of using all your senses to rehearse your sport in your mind. In this exercise I will ask you to practice visualizing your goals. Use the step by step process to guide you through the practice of visualization.

DID YOU KNOW?: Visualizing your goals helps reduce fear and anxiety, boosts confidence, increases motivation, strengthens muscle memory and motor contrl, and aids in overcoming the fear of failure.

Step 1:

Think about your **performance or process goal**. Where are you at? What do you see? What do What do you hear (ball bouncing)? What does it smell like? Think about the feeling of your jersey on your skin, the grooves of the basketball in your hands. How do you feel (energized)? What emotions are you feeling (confidence, excitement, joy).

Step 2:

Now find a quiet place and relax (take deep breaths). You can be sitting in a chair or laying on the floor or in the bed when doing this exercise.

Step 3:

Close your eyes and imagine yourself successfully completing your **performance or process goal**. Include all the senses mentioned in step 1. Try to make your image as vivid and detailed as possible, being sure to incorporate the emotion you will feel in that moment. Do this for 2 to 5 minutes.

NOTE: Visualization is just like any skill and requires practice and consistency. We recommend visualizing your performance or process goal for 2-5 minutes visualizing is daily, multiple times a week, and especially on game day.

Summary

Goal setting is a widely used mental skill among athletes. However, the key to success lies in understanding how to use them effectively and applying best practices. Throughout this chapter, you've learned how to apply outcome, performance, and process goals. You've learned to make your goals SMART: specific, measurable, action-oriented, realistic, and time-bound. Additionally, you've gained insights into best practices, understanding the do's and don'ts for goal setting. Lastly, you've discovered the importance of not only setting and planning for goals but also visualizing yourself successfully accomplishing them.

It's crucial to remember that accomplishing your goal requires repetition, consistency, discipline, and commitment. Setting the goal is the first step; you still have to put in the work required to accomplish it. Fortunately, after completing this chapter, you have the foundation equipped with the tools to successfully accomplish your goals.

THIS WEEKS ACTION PLANS

Please apply the goal setting strategies you learned this week to practice and competition using the action plans below.

1. **Awareness Exercise**

   Now that you've set your goals, pay attention to how they make you feel. Are you motivated? How has incorporating process goals into your routine impacted your performance? Gauge your level of focus and confidence. Assess if you have the resources and effort required to accomplish the goals you've set, so you can determine if they are realistic, attainable, or if they need to be adjusted.

2. **Practice Plan**

   Implement your goal setting strategy into your practice plan. For example, incorporate your process goals in your practice routine. If you're unable to, make sure you are setting aside time every week to work towards accomplishing your goal. Then determine if any adjustments need to be made towards.

3. **Game-Time Application**

   During your pregame routine, reflect on your performance goals. Implement game plan strategies that you have worked on all week in practice. Trust your skills and training, knowing that you've put in the work. After the game, reflect on whether you accomplished your performance goal. Consider if it needs adjustment or what you can do differently to ensure you achieve your performance goal in the next game. If you were successful at accomplishing your goal, note what you did well so you can continue to apply those same practices. Don't forget to celebrate the small wins and successes in practices or games.

MENTAL GAME ASSESSMENT CHAPTER 10

After your practice or competition this week, please answer a few questions about your mental game. It's best if you answer them on the same day as your scrimmage or game.

1. What were two things you did well this week with your goal setting approach in practice or competition?

2. What are two goal setting things you would like to improve for the next week's practice?

3. How dedicated were you to applying your goal-setting strategies? Did you allocate time towards achieving your goal? (Rate yourself on a scale of 1 - 10, where 1 is no effort made and 10 is giving 100% effort, implementing every strategy).

4. How effectively did you concentrate on the process goals? What obstacles hindered you from incorporating your goals into your practice or game routine?

5. How has your goal impacted your mental performance? (I feel confident, focus, motivated, giving more effort, seeing improvement, etc.)

6. How did i celebrate progress made or accomplishing daily or weekly goals?

7. Based on your answers to the questions above, how can you improve my goal setting skills for next week? Do I need to make any adjustments? If so list them below.

GOALSTRACKER

MONTH:
YEAR:

My Top Three Goals	
1	
2	
3	

To Do List

-
-
-
-
-

Action Plan

STEP 5

STEP 4

STEP 3

STEP 2

STEP 1

Rewards	1	2	3	4

HABIT TRACKER

"Your habits will determine your future."

Instructions: List your top 5 goals (process or performance) and check off or mark with an "X" each day you successfully complete the process goal in practice. At the end of the week or month, review your tracker. See which habits you consistently completed and where you might need to improve. Place your habit tracker in a location where you'll see it regularly, such as on your refrigerator, bathroom mirror, or locker-room. This visual reminder can help keep you accountable.

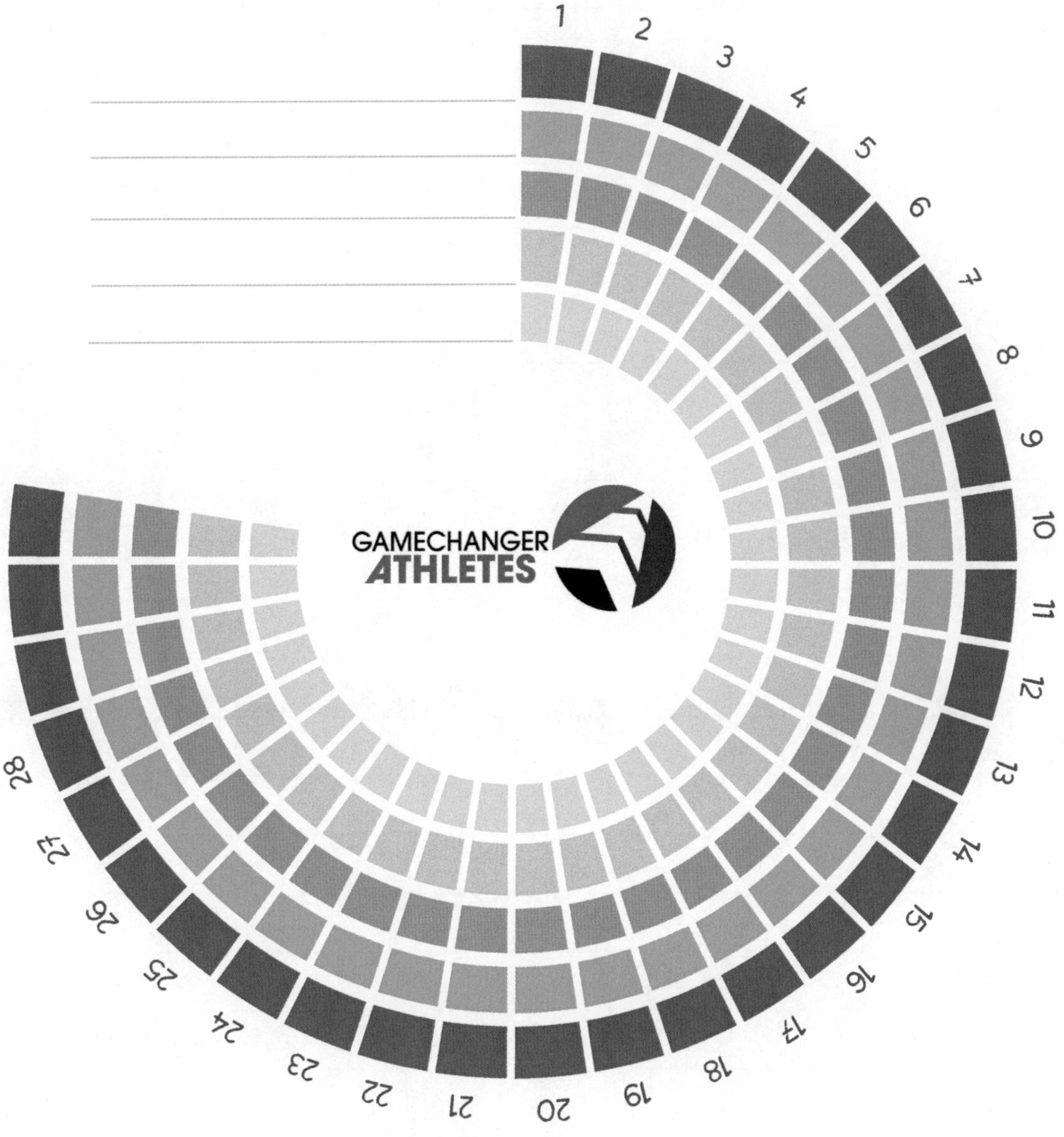

____

____

____

____

____

1 2 3 4 5 6 7 8 9 10 11 12 13 14 15 16 17 18 19 20 21 22 23 24 25 26 27 28 29 30 31

GAMECHANGER ATHLETES

MY NOTES

MY NOTES

MY NOTES

MY NOTES

MY NOTES

Made in the USA
Las Vegas, NV
14 March 2024